Go Thunk Yourself!™

Self-help Techniques

Become Rich, Famous, A Success.

With bonus references:

<u>As a Man Thinketh</u>, by James Allen
A Summary of <u>The Science of Getting Rich</u>, by Wallace D. Wattles
<u>Master Key System</u> Study Questions with Answers
by Charles F. Haanel

(See the end pages for more books in this series.)

Copyright © 2006 by Robert C. Worstell. All rights reserved.

No part of this publication may be reproduced, stored in a retrieval system, or transmitted in any form or by any means, electronic, mechanical, photocopying, recording, scanning, or otherwise, except as permitted under Section 107 or 108 of the 1976 United States Copyright Act, without the prior written permission of the Author.

Limit of Liability/Disclaimer of Warranty: While the publisher and the author have used their best efforts in preparing this book, they make no representations or warranties with respect to the accuracy or completeness of the contents of this book and specifically disclaim any implied warranties of merchantability or fitness for a particular purpose. No warranty may be created or extended by sales representatives or written sales materials. The advice and strategies contained herein may not be suitable for your situation. You should consult with a professional where appropriate. Neither the publisher nor the author shall be liable for any loss of profit or any other commercial damages, including but not limited to special, incidental, consequential, or other damages.

Beta release 0.85

"Go Thunk Yourself!" and the Go Thunk Yourself logo are trademarks of author Robert C. Worstell.

Publisher: Midwest Journal Press; ISBN: 978-0-6151-4121-3

Go Thunk Yourself!™

Self-help Techniques

Become Rich, Famous, A Success.

You can learn secrets used for centuries
to acquire money, power, success!

Follow this simple 14-day plan to become rich, famous,
and a success on your own.

by Dr. Robert C. Worstell

beta release .85

Includes bonus references:

As a Man Thinketh, by James Allen
A Summary of **The Science of Getting Rich**, by Wallace D. Wattles
Master Key System Study Questions with Answers
by Charles F. Haanel

First in a series – see end pages for more books by this author.

Dr. Robert C. Worstell

Table of Contents

Part I – How to "Thunk" Yourself..1
    Introduction...1
        Day 1 - REASON: 9
            Day 1 – Exercises..13
        Day 2 - THINK: 15
            Day 2 – Exercises..19
        Day 3 - CHANGE 21
            Day 3 – Exercises..27
        Day 4 - MIND: 29
            Day 4 – Exercises:...35
        Day 5 - ACHIEVE: 37
            Day 5 – Exercises..45
        Day 6 - POSITIVE: 47
            Day 6 – Exercises..53
        Day 7 - GOLDEN RULE: 55
            Day 7 – Exercise:...61
        Day 8 - VISION: 63
            Day 8 – Exercise:...67
        Day 9 - ACTION: 71
            Day 9 – Exercise:...77
        Day 10 - FAITH: 79
            Day 10 – Exercises:...85
        Day 11 - AFFIRMATION: 87
            Day 11 – Exercise:...91
        Day 12 - POWER THROUGH PRAYER: 93
            Day 12 – Exercises:...99
        Day 13 - PEACE: 101
            Day 13 – Exercise:...107
        Day 14 - MASTER MIND: 109
            Day 14 – Exercises:...113
    Summary: 115
    Appendix A:...123
    Appendix B:...129
    Appendix C:...133
    Addendum..137

Part II – The Original Study..145

The Search for an Underlying Core System..........146
    Introduction..........147
    Review of Literature..........149
        I. The Basis of This Study..........149
        II. Brief History and Apparent Origin
        of American Self-Help Classics..........157
    Findings..........161
    Discussion..........169
    Summary and Conclusions..........174
    Bibliography..........177

Part III – Bonus Section..........179
    As A Man Thinketh..........181
        Forward..........182
        Chapter One..........183
        Chapter Two..........187
        Chapter Three..........199
        Chapter Four..........203
        Chapter Five..........207
        Chapter Six..........211
        Chapter Seven..........217
    A Summary of The Science of Getting Rich..........221
    Master Key System..........225

Who is Dr. Robert C. Worstell?..........264

Other books in this series:..........265

More Resources From this Author:..........266

Books in the Go Thunk Yourself
Reference Library:..........268

Part I – How to "Thunk" Yourself...

Introduction

"God helps them who help themselves."
Benjamin Franklin – The Way to Wealth

Learning how to "thunk" is quite simple. In fact, you do it all the time – it's a native function. What I cover here is the key secrets of self-help that all bestselling authors agree on. Once you've studied this book, you'll see how all the rest of the bestselling self-help books simply tell you different parts of the same scene. In other words, they are selling you just a few points of "thunking" which people do natively anyway. Through this book, I'll give you the key 14 points of self-help "thunking" so that you can use these age-old techniques and improve your life.

So why did I need to write a book and why do you need to read it? Because all these guys tell you bits and pieces of the same current of thought. They all have the same system, but no one has put it into one single place before. Most of this is common sense, but unless you know the whole scene, you don't get the complete result.

But your result is up to you. Nothing is achieved without investment; there are no free rides, free lunches or lottery winnings without something being done or given in advance or in return.

Dr. Robert C. Worstell

Another phrase, time-worn: You get out what you put into it. So this book guarantees nothing. Results will vary from person to person, just as hair, eye and skin color aren't perfectly identical in any two people, even twins. This book only gives you an option to do something about anything you would like to improve in your life, from an extreme of getting outrageously wealthy to simply getting along better with a loved one or an enemy. People who want to change something in their lives will find some way to do it. This book is nothing but an introduction into the vast field of self-help or self-improvement.

It became necessary to write this book after a study was undertaken of several successful self-help books written as far as 6 centuries apart. This was when a small set of principles showed up in every single book. All of the books in this study were successful when first published and are being reprinted and sold today, some of them hundreds of years after their authors died. That was the criterion: they had to be still in circulation or best sellers long after their authors died – showing that people generally still found them useful and workable, not dependent on the personal magnetism of the author. Then some best-selling modern self-help books were reviewed as a cross-check of the accuracy of these points. The common points that each had were summarized and included in this text, modernized and made simpler to remember and use. The book was written in a modern style to make it simpler to read and understand.

I don't have to tell you these will give you success. That the majority of these books have been continual best-sellers for as many as 90 years or more proves people have found them useful and applicable.

There are hundreds of thousands, if not untold millions of people who have improved their lives or gotten prosperous from using these principles, many even before you or I were born. I really bring nothing new to this world with this writing, only putting it all in one spot and giving you a simple system to apply these to your lives. This book's system of distilled principles will work as much as you put yourself behind them and you will get out only in proportion to what you put in to your study, your application and your doggedness in seeing this through.

As I've said before, this book is just a mere introduction to the common system of self-help subject as described by the referenced authors. All the references I've used to boil down these basic points to their system are listed in the appendix at the back of this book. You can and should read these yourself to further your own understanding and ability in the area(s) you've chosen to improve. All are available on the Internet in one form or another and many are still being actively published today.

How to get the most out of this book.

There are three commonly known approaches to study:

1. Study with a purpose in mind – what are you trying to get out of this book? Why are you reading this instead of watching TV, listening to music or doing your homework?

2. Don't go past anything that doesn't make sense. While some things you have to accept on faith for the moment while the author then gets on with explaining it or giving examples, watch out for things like oddball nomenclature or technical terms which look and sound weird to begin with. But don't let that throw you off. You can always look up what the author said through a dictionary, and maybe a thesaurus and/or small encyclopedia. The important point is to understand what the person is trying to say. But if that author is simply illogical or inane, then do your own research. Maybe some points have some sense to them, but the writer came up with an nonsense conclusion. As well, a reader or author can words in the wrong usage or describe something inaccurately. Look, you're the reader – in the final analysis, it has to make sense to you. That applies to this book or any other.

3. Make sure you can apply it as you go. While some textbooks (and professors) make their readers swallow a huge amount of theory before they get to (if they ever do) some real use you can put this stuff to, it's often best to work out examples for yourself as you read. This keeps it in the real category, not the "I'll probably never use this anyway" back-burner section of your mind. So if you get to a point where you can't actually put it to any use, go back over the earlier sections to see where it quit making sense, sort that out, and then come forward. You might have to sketch it out or make some notes for yourself to do this sorting. As has been noted by various

education and self-help professionals, doing is the best way to learn – in addition to reading or studying.

Dale Carnegie also boiled it down quite simply at the beginning of one of his Public Speaking books:

"In order to get the most out of this book and to get it with rapidity and dispatch, do these four things:

"a. Start with a strong and persistent desire. . . .

"b. Prepare. . . .

"c. Act confident. 'To feel brave,' advises Professor William James, 'act as if we were brave, use all of our will to that end, and a courage fit will very likely replace the fit of fear.'

"d. Practice."

These apply to learning about self-help in more ways than you can imagine. A great deal of these applications will be explained or pointed out as we go through this book. But the above advice also applies to many different in-life situations, such as learning to drive a car or taking a college course.

The other point is that this book is not just read it and stash it. The best use for this book is to:

1. Read one chapter a day, plus any relevant section of the referenced authors for that day,

2. Do the exercises each day,

3. Finish the book by reading each chapter and summary,

4. Start over, repeating 1-3.

The reason for this is that repetition enables you to be more sure of being able to apply what you've studied and also to see the results as you go along. The exercises are written on a gradual slope of increasing difficulty and improved ability. When you finish off the book and start doing the first exercises again, you now will get much more out of the exercises, since you are coming back to them at a new, higher level of understanding and ability.

You can get also more out of this book by reading the other authors listed while or after you read this book. I'm not published by these book publishers, and most of the referenced authors have been dead for some time (excepting only one) so I don't get a dime from sending anyone their way. Simply, this is an introductory book, a summation of what these other authors researched. It's usually best to get the original data from the original sources. This book is just to tell you who to look up on what subject, so you don't have to burn needless months and years of your own life winding your way on false leads trying to get out of the labyrinth.

Self-help is an evolving subject. There have been many changes over the years and more will be coming. Here I hope you get a thorough introduction to the heavy-weights in the field and get well-started on your own journey of self-improvement.

So: Good luck.

As the Irish saying goes,

"May the road rise up to meet you on your journey."

Dr. Robert C. Worstell

Day 1 - REASON:

A reason to change, something to shoot for, goal.

> *"There are three types of people in this world:
> those who make things happen,
> those who watch things happen
> and those who wonder what happened."*
> Mary Kay Ash

Before anything can change, there needs to be a reason for change. Nothing in this universe is unmotivated, if only by the need for entertainment or distraction from boredom.

I take it that you picked up this book to get something out of it. There must then be something in your life that you would like to improve upon.

Do you always have enough spending money? Are you successful in life in every direction you attempt? Are you happy constantly, making friends easily and forming many deep, trusting relationships as a result?

Maybe you'd simply like to kick a bad habit, or get over a loss, or lose a few pounds.

All these things are possible to you, providing you want to change.

Right now, write down in the margin of this book – or one of the back pages or a separate page – exactly what it is that you want to change. You can always modify this later or change it to something entirely different if you want to. That is the premise of self-help: you can change something about your life if you want to.

Maybe, as a result of this book, you'll have such success with improving that item that you want to go ahead and change something else. With this book, or the books referenced in the back, you'll certainly be able to.

But it starts with deciding that something needs to be improved and exactly what that is. Now, if you haven't written that something down somewhere, do it now.

There's one caveat to know before starting this journey of self-improvement:

You can't get without giving.

Just as there is truly no free lunch or free beer, so any idea that just by reading a book you are going to get better without doing something yourself is a false one. Life itself has the lesson that you get out what you put in. The more you want to work at something, the better you will get at it. Musicians practice daily. Sport stars practice daily. Actors rehearse over and over, even after they have memorized their lines to perfection, even though they've given the show time after time for weeks. Practice makes perfect.

And so it is with any self-help or self-improvement activity. One must take personal responsibility for one's condition. Through this book, we'll go over the theory and reality of why this is so. One could always sue a fast-food chain for one's condition, but practically that will only get you money, not any improved condition. If you want to lose weight, go on a diet and stick to a sensible plan of meals once you are down to the weight you want. If you want to gain weight, there are many programs which will tell you to go to a gym and exercise, plus eat more protein. But these changes only start with you making a conscious decision to do something about your own condition.

You don't have to have a dire condition or take drastic, emergency actions to change it. But you do have to realize that in order to improve a condition, you are personally going to have to take responsibility for handling it, regardless of how you got that way. That is always the first step, which follows from noticing that you have a condition you'd like to change.

Dr. Robert C. Worstell

Through this book, we'll cover various exercises and techniques you can use to do something about your chosen area to improve. While it will be up to you to make the changes, we will have already done the homework to make sure that the techniques have been uncovered and point out additional resources you can study to find out more if you feel you need to.

But you'll get out what you put into it. That is the only guarantee we can make.

Day 1 – Exercises

Try this –

1. Take what you wrote down and put it on a card. Now turn that card over and write that same phrase in the past tense: instead of, "I'd like to have a new car," write "I have a new car." Put that card on your nightstand so you see it last thing at night and first thing in the morning. If you can, write another card and take it to where you work so you can keep this in mind in spare moments during the day. (We'll cover why you're doing this later. For now, we need to get the object you are trying to improve out there in front of you so you can study the rest of this book.

2. Select a room where you can be alone and undisturbed. Sit in a comfortable chair, erect – do not lounge. Let your thoughts roam as they will, but be perfectly still from 15 minutes to a half-hour. Practice in this daily will enable you to start controlling your body its physical area.

3. Next, in the same chair, be perfectly still, but allow the muscles in the body to relax, along with every nerve until you feel more quiet and restful. Mastering this will become easier as you practice it, enabling you to apply it while at work or at home, making life easier to appreciate and enjoy.

These exercises form the basis of a regular regimen which can bring about much improved conditions in your life, based entirely on how much you'd like to change your life around. We'll be adding to these drills as we go, so realize that you have plenty of chance to practice at them and get better – you don't have to be perfect the first day.

Many of these exercises come from Charles F. Haanel's work, <u>The Master Key System</u>. See the appendix for this and other books which can help you with the self improvement you are looking for. This book is the merest introduction to a very wide and broad topic. These exercises are culled from many sources, Haanel being a key one.

Have fun!

Day 2 - THINK:

You can think for yourself.

*"Minds are like parachutes;
they work best when open."*
- Thomas Dewar

Here's the choice in your life: think for yourself or think the way someone else wants you to. News media, advertisers, salespeople – these all want to have you think their way or no way, or at least that's the way they sound and look. This doesn't mean they're right, far from it. By survey, most people don't really trust these people to do their thinking for them.

But who is telling people to think for themselves or teach them how to do it? Certainly not the public schools and colleges, which have their own agenda through the books, teachers and administration. These are far from impartial.

Yet, there comes a time in almost everyone's life where a personal situation shows up and some original thinking is required. Or even in retrospect, one finds out (or has is pointed out to him/her) that a better decision could have been made.

The trick here is to figure out when you are thinking and when you are being made to think. Try this:

Try not to think of a pink elephant.

Now, most people immediately have a pink elephant show up, or some faint impression of one. This is a ploy of advertising and news media, schooling, etc. through their "subliminal advertising" and psychological study groups. Even churches, through their hired PR firms, are advertising this way. They give you opinions and reactions which you are supposed to spout back on cue. If they say buy a new car, you go out and mortgage the house or max out a credit card. If they say vote a certain way or that certain social programs are good or bad, then that is supposed to be your opinion or reaction.

But this isn't anywhere near the truth. Closer to truth is that many, many people give up their power of decision to these sources out of convenience, safety, loyalty, even friendship. People can still be loyal, safe and friends but retain their own power of decision and thought.

You can try this if you want:

Can you get an idea of a cat?

Now, who thought of that cat? That's right – you. You can have your own thoughts on just about anything. Probably you can think your own thoughts on anything. If not, practice will make it possible for you to think about anything that you want to.

As we'll cover later, doing your own thinking is directly related to changing your mind, which can help you improve that condition you wrote down on Day 1. I've meanwhile included some exercises in today's lesson which will help you improve your ability to think for yourself.

Dr. Robert C. Worstell

Day 2 – Exercises

Try this —

1. Get five pieces of paper.

Write numbers or letters on each one (your choice).

Now, turn them all face down.

Decide which one to turn up and turn that one up.

Then decide which one is next and turn that one up.

Do this for all the rest of them.

Here's the punchline: Who decided which one to turn up?

(You can do this as many times as you feel like it.)

2. Earlier we had you practice sitting still and relaxing. Now, while sitting relaxed in a quiet room, just look over the thoughts that are coming through your mind. You don't have to do anything with them, just see the variety of thoughts that are happening.

3. Next, try thinking no thoughts. This seems impossible at first – you will only get better with practice at this. Perhaps at first you'll only be able to go seconds without some other thought crowding in; practice will lengthen this. The reason for this is to demonstrate to you that thoughts are controllable, as well as to practice getting them under control. I've found that simply listening to your own breathing or pulse, or the sounds in the room – not thinking anything, just listening – can help you control these thoughts.

Do these for 15 minutes or a half-hour, preferably at the same time and place daily. In our next day's lesson and exercises, we'll add to the skills you've already started developing.

Day 3 - CHANGE

A person can change his own attitudes

"Men acquire a particular quality by constantly acting a particular way...
you become just by performing just actions,
temperate by performing temperate actions,
brave by performing brave actions."
- Aristotle

This idea Aristotle refers to shows up preeminently in Dale Carnegie's book, How to Develop Self-Confidence and Influence People by Public Speaking. He mentions here that confidence as a speaker can be achieved by simply changing the actions one does and the emotion will follow. He quotes William James (from his work The Gospel of Relaxation):

"Action seems to follow feeling, but really action and feeling go together; and by regulating the action, which is under the more direct control of the will, we can indirectly regulate the feeling, which is not.

"Thus the sovereign voluntary path to cheerfulness, if our spontaneous cheerfulness be lost, is to sit up cheerfully and to act and speak as if cheerfulness were already there. If such conduct does not make you feel cheerful, nothing else on that occasion can.

"So, to feel brave, act as if we were brave, use all of our will to that end, and a courage fit will very likely replace the fit of fear".

James himself refers to contemporary scientists who had studied this phenomenon. More recently many studies have been reported which have verified this to be correct in clinical studies and applied uses. People who before were not even able to experience many emotions were able to start relaxing once they practiced smiling.

Norman Cousins, in his book, <u>Anatomy of an Illness</u>, describes using humor as a means to overcome a degenerative disease which had left him all but paralyzed and with only a few months to live. Not only did he live, but recovered full use of his body and returned to work for a major New York magazine.

My own experience with this was in using this datum of smiling daily, whether I felt like it or not, for over a year. This was as part of a test of this datum, as well as finding out that it was a great deal more fun at my job when I smiled and tried to cheer people up regardless of how I or they felt that day or at the time. At the end of that year, I compared notes and found that I was more routinely cheerful and optimistic than I had felt the year before. It had become a habit of mine to be cheerful, optimistic and more outgoing. Where before this test started, I was still a bit shy, reserved and sometimes moody. I had participated in no training or counseling during that period, so the results were simply as a result of my self-enforced and practiced "smiling routine."

This single point is one of the few key building blocks of any self-help. It is a method where you can prove to yourself that any emotion you are experiencing can be brought under control and changed at will. We'll try it as part of our exercises today, later, so you can prove this to yourself.

The mental state of a person will affect the decisions he/she makes in life. Feelings of hopelessness will result in apathetic decisions to do nothing about it and be a victim. Fear will prompt a person to simply retreat from doing anything, or take the easiest, less painful way out. Anger might make a person decide to attack or criticize, saying things one might regret later on. The interested, even enthusiastic person will decide in terms of the best solution that benefits the majority concerned – he/she might even work out how to make a profit off the deal!

Many people have regretted some major decision in life and have had this worry them from that point on. Norman Vincent Peale, in his best seller <u>The Power of Positive Thinking</u> has many chapters on how to improve one's outlook on life. In his chapter called "How to Break the Worry Habit," he suggests just before going to sleep at night to envision the mind as a basin and draining all worries by removing the stopper. He recommends going through this process five times at night to improve sleep.

As well, he says to do this several times in the middle of the day. His book is an excellent one in this particular area of positive thinking and I recommend it highly.

Another book which has been found by many to be very effective in this area is by Dale Carnegie, <u>How to Win Friends and Influence People</u>. While he has many, many points to cover, he begins the book by telling his readers that one of the most effective way to study is by doing, not simply being taught or reading. Doing is the way to really learn something well. In one of his chapters, he relates the value of a smile:

> *"Charles Schwab told me his smile had been worth a million dollars. And he was probably understating the truth. For Schwab's personality, his charm, his ability to make people like him, were almost wholly responsible for his extraordinary success; and one of the most delightful factors in his personality was his captivating smile."*

Wouldn't you like to have such a financially rewarding smile? People that are friendly toward you certainly are more favorable in signing business deals.

But life in general can be much more delightful if it is actively lead into a pleasant routine of smiling, cheerfulness, and delight in life itself.

If you find that you can change your attitude, you will see that you can change your own mind whichever way you want to. This will become more important later on when we bring in more advanced drills and techniques.

Day 3 – Exercises

Try this –

1. Smile. Walk around your home and simply smile at everything. It won't be long before you start noticing nice things about everything and everyone you smile at. Probably you'll quickly find yourself having a more cheerful attitude towards everything around you, that the problems you may have don't seem so pressing. Perhaps you might find better solutions than those you have thought up so far. Practice smiling first thing in the morning and after every meal. See how it makes you feel.

2. In your that room with the chair you've been using, sit and relax physically as you did in Day one. Now just as you let go physically, let go mentally of adverse mental conditions such as hatred, anger, worry, jealousy, envy, sorrow, trouble or disappointment. You can use Peale's solution above. Imagine that your mind is a big basin with a rubber stopper at the bottom. In your imagination, remove the stopper and see the thoughts, worries and troubles drain down until the basin is empty. Then start is all over and repeat this four more times.

3. During the following day, find a quiet moment at work or during the lunch hour where you can do the above exercise. Practice will make this easier and quicker to do. Try to do this several times each day, until it becomes a simple habit of choice to rid troublesome thoughts from your attitudes and to control your attitude to a more positive outlook.

Day 4 - MIND:

The surrounding environment is a result of the mental environment.

"In the province of the mind, what one believes to be true either is true or becomes true." – John Lilly

Let's recap what we've covered in the last three days:

- There's a reason you're studying this book.
- You can think for yourself.
- You can change your own attitude on your own.

If you've tried these out for yourself by doing the exercises and found them to be true, then the next datum I'm about to tell you should seem logical:

The physical environment around you can be changed by changing your mental environment.

To backtrack a bit, just suppose, when you weren't feeling very good, someone came up with a problem that demanded an immediate solution. The solution you came up with wasn't the best and perhaps it had drawbacks, but was the best you could come up with on short notice, under the circumstances. Now you have to explain that decision to your boss or to the Board.

Now suppose you were feeling great that day, ready to take on the world, at your physical and mental best. This same someone came up with the same problem, still demanding a solution. The solution could be thought out faster, more details could be included, a more optimal result was produced. Better for the company and better for your job. You get kudos for this and perhaps even a raise for saving the company money.

The difference in these two scenarios was your attitude, not the problem. Now you know that, with practice, you could adopt any attitude at all towards that problem, toward your job, toward the company. Now every day can be a great day. Every solution can be optimal for all concerned. This logical argument above is just the tip of the iceberg as far as your mental condition affecting your environmental scene.

The precise details of how this is accomplished is best covered by Charles F. Haanel in his book, <u>The Master Key System</u> . As well, a more succinct version is found in James Allen's <u>As a Man Thinketh</u>. Both of these books cover the technical and philosophic details behind self-improvement and outline the exact ways that the way you set your mind predicts the outcome of your personal environment.

This might fly in the face of some modern thought about minds, genetics, fate, destiny and various other subjects. But you are here to change somethings about your life, not get into the scientific and philosophical background arguments. (Frankly, if you wanted to, you can find scientific studies which exactly support each point that Haanel or any of these other referenced self-help authors stated. But unless you have the time to verify these books' premise by finding these supportive studies or to repeating these authors' research and readings, just for now accept that the technology of this is very precise and has been noted by scientists back as early as 1909 and philosophers in the 14th century and before, back to Plato and Aristotle at least.)

What and how one thinks changes and even forms the environment around one.

You've already seen this in your own attitudes. The trick on this is to take it further and work out what else you would like to change in the world around you. Using the tools you already have read and practiced, try taking responsibility for and changing your attitude toward something you'd like to improve in your life. While this may or may not make for immediate changes, you may find some different ways of dealing with some person or problem in your life.

James Allen covers this idea simply:

> *"Man is buffeted by circumstances so long as he believes himself to be the creature of outside conditions, but when he realizes that he is a creative power, and that he may command the hidden soil and seeds of his being out of which circumstances grow; he then becomes the rightful master of himself."*

That is the core and substance before you. Your attitudes and collective understandings about the world around you are what factually determine what and how things happen around you. We've already seen how you can change your own attitude and how such a changed attitude might change the outcome of your decisions. The further step to take, logically, is that the combined experiences from your learning, education, parental examples, TV, news, social groups – all these give you basic ideas that you can either use or discard as you see fit. But the ones you decided were worth keeping are the ones which now tell you how to act, what to do, what emotions are "correct" or "appropriate" for any given situation, etc., because you keep them there and keep using them.

If you are serious about self-improvement, or self-help, take this piece of advice: change your mind. Start thinking about how you currently react to things and sort these out against whether you think these reactions are sensible or based on common sense. If some sort of action is illogical, try simply working out what a more positive, more constructive reaction would be. Practice saying or doing that in your mind and even practice out loud, if you wish. The next time such a situation could occur, you'll be ready.

Steven Covey, in his bestselling <u>The 7 Habits of Highly Effective People</u> covers it simply:

"The ability to subordinate an impulse to a value is the essence of the proactive person. Reactive people are driven by feelings, by circumstances, by conditions, by their environment. Proactive people are driven by values – carefully thought about, selected and internalized values.

"Proactive people are still influenced by external stimuli, whether physical, social, or psychological. But their response to the stimuli, conscious or unconscious, is a value-based choice or response."

Again, we come to the notice I made in the introduction: This book is an introduction to a common system of self-help. Not in one day was the universe created or Rome built. We are going to cover a great deal more tools which will enable you to make these choices. Covey has himself developed very good advice; if you dropped this book now and picked his up, you'd be no worse off. As well, you could study Carnegie or Hill or Haanel and probably come up with similar results.

What I am doing with this book is to show you a brief introduction to these authors and the common principles of self-help. I am laying out here the key points and substance of their knowledge in a logical pattern. Trying to change your whole life overnight probably wouldn't be the easiest thing you've ever tried – it could be done, but not easily. This book lays out simple explanations and equally simple, but powerful drills in a sequence where results can be achieved through repetitive and cyclical use.

In this day's study, we are covering the mind's effect on the environment. So let's do some exercises to see if we can't get more causative over them by changing our mind.

Day 4 – Exercises:

Try this –

We've now learned to relax, physically and mentally, and to empty our minds of destructive thoughts. Now we need to start placing positive thoughts and attitudes there.

1. In the same room and chair as before, think of a place which has pleasant associations. Try to form a complete mental image picture of it. This won't necessarily be easy at first, but practice will bring about more and more complete and vivid versions of that scene for you.

2. Next, try concentrating on a single thought for 1o minutes. Bring a photograph with you and study the face carefully. Note the expression, the shape of the nose, position of the eyebrows, the clothing and hair arrangement – all the details of it. Now, close your eyes and try to see it mentally for yourself. Again, this is a skill to acquire and the more you do it, the easier it will become. See if you can hold the thought for 10 minutes. More than likely your mind will wander at first, but keep at it for 10 minutes.

Day 5 - ACHIEVE:

Personal control is possible over being, doing, achieving and acquiring.

"Whether you believe you can do a thing or not, you're right."
- Henry Ford.

OK, so now we know and have experienced being able to change our attitudes and control what goes on in our own mind. What I tell you next has been in every self-help book I've opened and is applicable to every person on this planet, regardless of religious beliefs, sex or philosophy:

You can achieve anything you want to; the only limits are what you've set for yourself.

True. Start picking up the books I've already mentioned, or as noted in the appendix, and you'll see it for yourself. Or start roaming through biographies of people who have achieved great things, made a fortune (or several) or were famous for one or more other reasons. Before they started their climb, you'll find some attitude they had which enabled them to overcome any challenge or adversity. Many blind musicians have overcame discrimination and disabilities to become successful and wealthy. College drop-outs currently operate some of the biggest and most financially successful corporations in this county. America is built on the dream of any immigrant or native-born person being able to achieve whatever they wanted and then actually doing it. Modern entertainers are nearly all of this cut, making their way from obscurity to fame and fortune; very few were already rich and famous before they started singing or acting.

You can change anything in your life that you want to. It's all in your own state of mind.

Let's look a bit more in detail how this is accomplished:

- More opportunity does or doesn't present itself and is taken advantage of or passed by.
- A person thinks – in one's own control or not,
- That person's mind is "made up," it becomes fixed in a series of attitudes as solutions for various situations he/she faces.
- The behavior and personality of that person is then determined and becomes practiced, "set in their ways."
- Opportunities then come about (or not) because that person seeks them or lets them go. "Luck" is good or bad or indifferent in this same scheme.
- The person has or doesn't have the perseverance and attention to detail/professional attitude to perform exceptionally well at what he/she does.

All of this is dependent on the original thinking done to begin with. However, you also see by this point that nothing is "cast in stone" as regards mental state or condition. People maintain, improve or degrade their image of themselves continually during their lives. What we think determines our personality, our achievements and our future or lack of it. Today's failure can become tomorrow's success and vice-versa.

James Allen points this out eloquently in his short text from 1902,

"A man's mind may be likened to a garden, which may be intelligently cultivated or allowed to run wild; but whether cultivated or neglected, it must, and will bring forth. If no useful seeds are put into it, then an abundance of useless weed-seeds will fall therein, and will continue to produce their kind. Just as a gardener cultivates his plot, keeping it free from weeds, and growing the flowers and fruits which he requires so may a man tend the garden of his mind, weeding out all the wrong, useless and impure thoughts, and cultivating toward perfection the flowers and fruits of right, useful and pure thoughts. By pursuing this process, a man sooner or later discovers that he is the master-gardener of his soul, the director of his life. He also reveals, within himself, the flaws of thought, and understands, with ever-increasing accuracy, how the thought-forces and mind elements operate in the shaping of character, circumstances, and destiny."

All great corporations were built on the leadership and inspiration of single persons who had confidence in themselves and their actions. This confidence was self-created and self-recognized. In any such successful company, you never see a "puppet" in some CEO or Board Chairman position who is told by some other person how to act and what decision to make. CEO's got there because they think they can do something and do.

That is the key – their own thoughts.

And any such success can be yours. You just have to be willing to change your thoughts and then do it.

There are a few more details to it, more tools that we will be bringing to you to study in succeeding chapters, but the steps to study here are these:

- Thought creates the state of mind.
- Mind monitors personality.
- Personality affords personal success or lack of it.

Or in other words,

- A person can control his own thoughts.
- So one can improve his attitudes and so his personality.

- And so, attain success from the same available factors in his/her life, or new factors which then accrue.

Steven Covey covers this in some detail in his <u>7 Habits</u> book, giving very thorough theory and practical examples of how and why this occurs. More examples can be found in Dr. Peale's book.

Napoleon Hill precedes both of these with his <u>Think and Grow Rich</u>. Hill was working as a reporter and was assigned to do a series of articles on successful people. He first interviewed Andrew Carnegie. This interview which normally would have taken only a few hours, took three days. At the end of that time, Mr. Carnegie commissioned Hill to interview over 500 millionaires to find a success formula that could be used by the average person. Some of these included Thomas Edison, Alexander Graham Bell, Henry Ford, Charles M. Schwab, Theodore Roosevelt, William Wrigley Jr, George Eastman, Woodrow Wilson, William H. Taft, John D. Rockefeller, F. W. Woolworth. The result was a book which took Hill over 20 years to research and write, but has gone on to sell over 7 million copies.

Hill gives this advice in improving persistence, a useful personality attribute:

"HOW TO DEVELOP PERSISTENCE

"There are four simple steps which lead to the habit of PERSISTENCE. They call for no great amount of intelligence, no particular amount of education, and but little time or effort. The necessary steps are:

"1. A DEFINITE PURPOSE BACKED BY BURNING DESIRE FOR ITS FULFILLMENT.

"2. A DEFINATE PLAN, EXPRESSED IN CONTINUOUS ACTION.

"3. A MIND CLOSED TIGHTLY AGAINST ALL NEGATIVE AND DISCOURAGING INFLUENCES, including negative suggestions of relatives, friends and acquaintances.

"4. A FRIENDLY ALLIANCE WITH ONE OR MORE PERSONS WHO WILL ENCOURAGE ONE TO FOLLOW THROUGH WITH BOTH PLAN AND PURPOSE."

You can see, using what we have already covered, these steps are pretty simply achieved by anyone who wants to improve their life and develop persistence, much less be successful, happy and/or wealthy in doing so.

You just have to "make up your mind" to do so and then do so.

Day 5 – Exercises

Try this –

1. Take that original idea which you wrote down on day one. This is something you wanted to accomplish or achieve or have.

a. Now, figure out what you would have to do to get this. This can be general terms right now – just an idea of the actions you are going to have to take to make this happen.

b. Then, once this list of things to do is complete, figure out what personality you would have to create or develop in order to do those actions.

c. Lastly, look around mentally and see if there are some thoughts or mental habits that might need to be changed in order for that personality to surface.

2. In Day 4, we visualized a photo of a friend or acquaintance. Sitting in that same chair, visualize this person completely, including the last conversation you had, what he looked like, how he dressed, his mannerisms. Now, in your mind, talk to him about some subject you are interested in and elicit his response. Can you get him excited about what you are talking about – do you see his eyes light up as he leans forward to find out all you have to say on the subject? This is the next step to improve on. You'll be achieving control over what you are thinking and creating in your own mind. This is an important skill which you'll develop more in the succeeding days of material coming up.

Day 6 - POSITIVE:

Emphasis on positive outlook on life – eliminating critical thought and behavior.

*"Smile and the world smiles with you,
frown and the world frowns upon you."*
– Unknown

This next set of actions to learn is no Quantum Leap of logic. You can change your attitudes, change your thought, change your mind and so your personality, actions and accomplishment level. You now know the basics of how to achieve or acquire anything you want – or could probably work out the rest.

What the rest of this book will tell you, then, are some pratfalls to avoid.

Creation is a positive action. Destruction, while considered negative action, is arguably lack of any positive action. So, with this logic, there is really only a brilliant white version of creative thought or action, along with varying shades of gray down to a completely black absence of creating in anyone's life, or any area of it. As well, non-positive thoughts would then be based on solutions for which a truly creative, optimal solution hasn't been found. Non-positive thought is just inefficient, carrying around old junk one has collected instead of making your own shiny new solutions and ideas. Some of this thinking can be attributed to simple lack of practice in thinking things through to their best solution, not uncommon in our TV-raised generations.

Such inefficient thought shows up as apparent stupidity, dullness or "blockheadedness". It's not that a person can't think, his/her mental efforts are slowed by having to think through solutions others have already achieved for themselves. This is why successful firefighters, soldiers, paramedics and other professionals can quickly solve any emergency situation in split-seconds – they have a massed storage of ready solutions available for instantaneous execution.

More commonly, the current culture tolerates critical remarks and snide comments as ways to confront something. Newscasting now deals with heightening the controversial rather than simply finding applicable facts. Good news (positively solved situations with optimal outcomes) are the rare gems on TV and radio these days. Practically, they have lost credibility and have become mere entertainment sources – just another stop on the hundred-channel sets so common today. Since they are so filled with non-positive slant, it is hard to work out a solution from the available data; it's no wonder that these news sources aren't "trusted" these days by any more than one-third of their own viewing public – and more often, people are switching to the Internet.

We've covered earlier the point of getting out of anything what you put into it. This applies to your attitude toward life as well. Go around being critical of others at your work place and you will quickly find out that they start being critical of you – if not to your face, then behind your back. Any cooperation you would like to have from them just vanished. Negative actions, give you negative feedback and results.

The same thing happens in your mind. People or areas you are critical of are not easily solved mentally as problems. Stephen Covey refers in his works to what he calls the "spiritual and emotional cancers" of criticizing, complaining, comparing and contending. When you compete with someone, more often than not, that person becomes your enemy. You are more interested in winning against him/her than in constructively finding ways where you can both win in the same field. If you fill your mind with enemies that you are constantly critical of, find fault with or compete with, then mentally you are constantly on the lookout to dodge potential attacks coming your way. So you can see how this could mire your mind down in a great deal or all your mental energies being used in fending off attacks from potential enemies.

Sales forces suffer from this. Unknowing managers pit them against each other for top sales prizes instead of getting them to cooperate with each other, such as trading tips or teamwork on a difficult prospect.

I knew a man who used his mind to build a multinational organization and become very rich. However, he always considered that he had to be the best at everything, repeating this statement to himself daily to make it become true. While a fine idea in itself, he also couldn't allow anyone to become better than he was, so mentally thought that people would attack him and try to bring him down as he was so "powerful". He started attacks against these potential "enemies" so that they couldn't get "power" over him, using his corporation's legal and PR resources. Because some of these actions themselves were illegal, harassment and slander law suits started mounting up. His solution was to go into seclusion, buying a remote ranch and allowing only a few people to attend to him, staying separate from his wife, children and long-time friends, communicating mostly by letter. While his corporation is still settling his/their suits at great expense to the corporation, he died alone with only a caretaker present – his whereabouts secret from anyone who truly loved him.

This is one of the pratfalls to avoid. While you can have all the money in the world, as the old saying goes, "you can't buy happiness." True wealth and prosperity is built on giving as well as receiving, on making sure that you are positively contributing to everyone around you. Two of the richest men on earth, forming a couple of the largest corporations that still exist were Ray Kroc (McDonald's) and Sam Walton (Wal-Mart). Both made more millionaires than they could keep track of. Walton even gave most of his wealth to his children on a routine basis – a fact that kept him off the "richest man on earth" list. Both decided early on to make a great product that was a bargain for the consumer. While there is always "trash-talking" going on about them and their companies, I invite you to read up on them, read their biographies and decide for yourself.

The richest do not hold wealth in stasis, they are just channels for it, as Haanel points out.

In order to truly succeed at improving you want to improve, you are going to have to eliminate any non-positive attitude, non-constructive attitude in the area you are trying to improve. Negative (or actually non-positive) thought is just a lot of excess baggage you are carrying around which is keeping you from really taking off. Success won't let you check those bags in – there's too many, they won't fit in the overhead or under the seat. The majority of leading self-help books cover this point, most of them over and over, that you are going to have to take responsibility for what you are thinking and actively change those thoughts. If you continue thinking the same way you have been all this time, then you'll be no closer to accomplishing whatever you wrote down in Day 1 than 10 years ago.

This book isn't breaking any new ground; I'm only reporting what others have already covered. These authors have done their own research and concluded this same point. Dr. Covey covers this in his book as "Habit 5 – Think Win-Win." Mr. Carnegie covers this point in his book in the Chapter entitled, "A Sure Way of Making Enemies – and How to Avoid It," which deals with the art of constructive criticism.

As far as a positive mindset as a means for getting wealthy, Wallace D. Wattles described it this way in his 1910 classic, <u>The Science of Getting Rich</u>:

> *"Moral and spiritual greatness is possible only to those who are above the competitive battle for existence; and only those who are becoming rich on the plane of creative thought are free from the degrading influences of competition. If your heart is set on domestic happiness, remember that love flourishes best where there is refinement, a high level of thought, and freedom from corrupting influences; and these are to be found only where riches are attained by the exercise of creative thought, without strife or rivalry."*

This can simply be done by those exercises you've already practiced so far, namely draining off all thoughts and replacing them with positive ones. We'll cover a few more exercises today which will augment these and help you improve your mind even more.

Day 6 – Exercises

Try this –

By this time, you've started having much more control over what goes through your mind. The next point to cover is to work on creative thought.

1. From Dr. Peale's book: "At intervals during the day practice thinking a carefully selected series of peaceful thoughts. Let mental pictures of the most peaceful scenes you have ever witnessed pass across your mind, as, for example, some beautiful valley filled with the hush of evening time, as the shadows lengthen and sun sinks to rest. Or recall the silvery light of the moon falling across rippling waters, or remember the sea washing gently upon soft shores of sand. Such peaceful thought images will work upon your mind as a healing medicine. So now and then during every day allow motion pictures of peace slowly to cross your mind.

2. "Practice the technique of suggestive articulation, that is, repeat audibly some peaceful words. Words have profound suggestive power, and there is healing in the very saying of them. Utter a series of panicky words and your mind will immediately go into a mild state of nervousness. You will perhaps feel a sinking feeling in the pit of your stomach that will affect your entire physical mechanism. If, on the contrary, you speak peaceful, quieting words, you mind will react in a peaceful manner. Use such a word as tranquility. Repeat that word slowly several times. Tranquility is one of the most beautiful and melodic of all English words, and the mere saying of it tend to induce a tranquil state. "

Day 7 - GOLDEN RULE:

Underlying moral/ethical understanding is the base for self-help

"Always treat others as you would like them to treat you."
- Jesus of Nazareth (Matthew 7:12)

As we've found that positive, creative thought is more vital, more effective than non-positive, non-creative thought – this leads logically to the next step: in order to make the best decisions, the most profitable ones, we have to treat others like we would like to be treated.

Wouldn't you like to be surrounded by cheerful people who are encouraging and creatively solving the problems life hands them? Remember that old adages we stated in an earlier section of this book:

You can't get without giving;

You'll only get out what you put in.

This culture, your mind, the environment surrounding you inexorably turns around according to this Golden Rule. This has been so long observed as true throughout history that nearly every religion has some version of it in their scriptures.

You can always try it for yourself. Go around and treat people with fairness, honesty, trust — all the virtues. Try this for a week and note the changes you make in your life. If this doesn't give you some significant changes, you can always try the reverse (but don't say I didn't warn you that this is a very effective way to ruin your life by cheating, lying, deceiving and generally mistreating your former friends). One more effective example is to take someone who is some "enemy" of yours and start treating him with respect, courtesy and fairness. It might take a while to get it through his head, but you'll see some amazing reactions from him. (One idea of what he's thinking is captured in the old phrase, "Smile. It makes them wonder what you've been up to.")

Again, the majority of these books cover this simple point:

You have to have an ethical base to your actions in order to maintain any forward progress.

There was an underlying reason to this book's research: to see if there were common system of proved self-help techniques. I started with only highly successful books that are even today being distributed, long after the author's death. These books all had common points. Distilled into a fourteen point series, they were then compared with more recent works, such as Dr. Covey's. Only his work made the "short list." Out of the fourteen points I distilled, one significant one was the mandatory use of such a character ethic or ethical/moral code in dealing with life.

Dr. Covey relates how he came to find this in the opening chapter of his book. He was researching 200 years of success literature in the United States, resolving what a democratic society considered to be keys to successful living. While his study covered literally hundreds of books, articles and essays on the subject, he found that there was a dividing line about 50 years ago. While the first 150 years was based on what he calls the Character Ethic, the last 50 years shifted over to what he calls the Personality Ethic.

The Personality Ethic was erected on image, behavior and human public relations and tended to culminate in shallow, trite aphorisms such as "Your attitude determines your altitude," and "Smiling wins more friends than frowning." These self-help books, tapes and pamphlets only worked to a certain degree and are widely lampooned because of their lack of underlying principles.

This was even known to the philosopher Al Ghazzali, in "The Alchemy of Happiness," probably the first known self-help work, written around the 14th century. Ghazzali mentions here how people he had observed would simply mouth the words of the Koran and other religious works as some sort of semi-automatic circuit which enabled them to live their lives and so obtain their success. But without understanding and utilizing the meaning behind the words, you might as well hire a Karaoke singer for your next big concert at Madison

Square Gardens. There's a wide difference between a trite phrase and the actual.

Dr. Covey describes the Character Ethic in his book:

> *"The Character Ethic taught that there are basic principles of effective living, and that people can only experience true success and enduring happiness as they learn and integrate these principles into their basic character."*

We are not interested in what is referred to in the music industry as "one shot wonders." Just as a simple coat of paint will not repair rotted siding on a building, this book covers not just how to be successful, get wealthy or happy, but the reasons behind why you do what you need to so you can make this a perpetual, ongoing habit in your life. The reason for this is logical and follows what we have covered so far. Let's chase this down:

- You have something you want to improve in your life.
- So you have to change your mind in order to make that happen.
- The most successful way to do this is a positive, creative one.
- To maintain a positive, creative approach to life, there must be an ethical, rational basis for making future decisions and thoughts. Otherwise, you would

simply drop back into old habits which created the scene you are now seeking to improve.

Dr. Covey's book is highly recommended in this particular vein. He covers simple habits that can be acquired through practice which in turn will start changing around your life and make such changes into an evolution of improvement for you. But he also gives the rational explanations of why his seven habits work, so you can continue to develop them in your own life and in your business or group.

If you already have a set moral or ethical base that is proving successful, I'm not telling you to abandon it in the next ditch you come to. However, character training in America has been weak and getting weaker for years. We now have experienced elected political leaders and church officials who have lied, deceived and acted in immoral ways, becoming top news makers in the media.

Without an ethical base, one is like a boat in a storm with no anchor, rudder or oars. If that boat is to make it through the storm without swamping, it would require a miracle. So it is in trying to make it through life with no basis for making decisions.

Many have worked out their ethical and moral system entirely based on the Golden Rule. Since this gives you a comparison, you can evaluate how you act against how you would like others to act around you. You don't like people who are inconsiderate of you, so try to be considerate of others. Manners evolved much in this fashion and continue to evolve. Making unusual noises at meal time, yelling or throwing tantrums – no one likes these. So people evolve etiquette in order to get along with each other.

People can also use this Golden Rule at work, where cooperation will get more work done than competition. This then gives you a working version that you can develop to work out how to treat people in positive, creative fashions. These actions will then return positive re-actions toward you.

Day 7 – Exercise:

Try this –

In your usual chair and room, try this exercise from Haanel's book:

"Visualize a plant; take a flower, the one you most admire, bring it from the unseen into the seen, plant the tiny seed, water it, care for it, place it where it will get the direct rays of the morning sun, see the seed burst; it is now a living thing, something which is alive and beginning to search for the means of subsistence. See the roots penetrating the earth, watch them shoot out in all directions and remember that they are living cells dividing and subdividing, and that they will soon number millions, that each cell is intelligent, that it knows what it wants and knows how to get it. See the stem shoot forward and upward, watch it burst through the surface of the earth, see it divide and form branches, see how perfect and symmetrical each branch is formed, see the leaves begin to form, and then the tiny stems, each one holding aloft a bud, and as you watch you see the bud begin to unfold and your favorite flower comes to view; and now if you will concentrate intently you will become conscious of a fragrance; it is the fragrance of the flower as the breeze gently sways the beautiful creation which you have visualized."

Day 8 - VISION:

Visions are composed of hopes and dreams; they create reality.

*"Obstacles are things a person sees
when he takes his eyes off his goal."*
- E. Joseph Cossman

Creating a vision, a goal to achieve is common to all these works; they sometimes differ in their terminology for them. Napoleon Hill mentions in the first paragraph of his book:

"TRULY, 'thoughts are things,' and powerful things at that, when they are mixed with definiteness of purpose, persistence, and a BURNING DESIRE for their translation into riches, or other material objects."

You have now been working for 7 days at the various exercises and ideas of this book – and perhaps have picked up and started reading some of the others I've referenced along the way. By now you have some idea of what you want to accomplish, how to change your thoughts and attitudes to positive ones in order to start achieving what you want out of life. As well, we have seen that an ethical basis will enable you to keep going on this route of self-improvement.

Let's now look at where you are going. Taking that one thing you want to achieve, you might be satisfied with this one improvement in your life. On the other hand, this might be the tip of a whole iceberg which is hidden unseen beneath the surface of the deep ocean of your mind.

Practically, the only limits in your mind are those you've accepted. Most consider that imagination can be boundless, capable of inventing or bringing anything into existence. So one can imagine boundaries and barriers which are impossible to overcome. By the same mental creativity, one could create the universal solvent, which nothing can hold as it dissolves everything it touches.

We've covered that as the mind is set, so the universe tends to respond. The difference with how well the universe responds is due to a few factors. Today we will cover vision – or lack of it – as a key factor.

Vision is simply more mental creation. But the scope of it is what we are discussing here. One can imagine simply receiving a hundred dollar bill. Now let's take this further: what are you going to do to receive that? (You can't get without giving.) What are the conditions of this? Do you get a check and cash it? Does this show up as a bonus in your pay check? Does one of your creditors simply show up with a payment? Or is this simply a gift from being nice to a loved one?

The vision is the most complete view of the whole scenario you are trying to achieve. It becomes a complete creation by building as you go. If you consider that you'd like to get your house refurbished, then work out all the details of exactly what type of carpet, paint, furniture, etc. you'd like to acquire. Work out the budget in your mind, considering all the tools and other hardware which will be necessary to install it with. Will you do it all yourself? Then you will have to consider having time to do it on weekends or other odd times. If you are going to get these professionally installed, then expand the budget to accommodate this. As you work over this vision, more and more details will be added as you go. The thing to do is to not hold back, but envision it as completely as possible.

Once you have it pretty much the way you want it, then consider it done. That is the key point. If you consider that you are going to get a hundred dollars, it will be true – you are always going to be "getting a hundred dollars," but that cash won't show up in front of you. The trick is to consider it already accomplished and in your possession. The more you creatively envision it, the more the environment will begin to comply.

You may think this is off-the-deep-end thinking. But carefully review the above: you have to give in order to get; you can't get something for nothing. How you consider you will be getting this also has to be part of the creative vision. Do you need to get a better-paying job? Do you need to work more efficiently at the one you have? Does this mean you will have to adopt an efficient, productive personality?

You could win it at the lottery. This will require buying tickets (at least one) and being very lucky. What are the personality attitudes and attributes of a lucky person? What do you plan to do with the money? Are you prepared for the taxes and other responsibilities? Do you consider that a lot of people will want to "hit you up" for contributions and donations to their cause (or pocket)? Think the thought through. Once you do, you can win all the money you want at any game you want. But the vision has to be there and has to be complete.

Once you start building your vision, simply keep at it, refining it, expanding its scope, working out how and who it will benefit, how to take care and maintain it, etc. Create away! Remember – there are no real limits except those you have accepted for yourself.

You're already well on your way to achieving anything you want in life with what we've already covered. Today's exercise will bring you closer, giving you some experience with creating a complete vision of what you want to achieve, acquire or have.

Day 8 – Exercise:

Try this –

This is again from Haanel's book. While he uses a battleship as an example, you could repeat the exercise with various other articles, such as a skyscraper, space rocket, video game or any thing that meets your fancy:

1. "Take the same position as heretofore and visualize a Battleship; see the grim monster floating on the surface of the water; there appears to be no life anywhere about; all is silence; you know that by far the largest part of the vessel is under water; out of sight; you know that the ship is as large and as heavy as a twenty-story skyscraper; you know that there are hundreds of men ready to spring to their appointed task instantly; you know that every department is in charge of able, trained, skilled officials who have proven themselves competent to take charge of this marvelous piece of mechanism; you know that although it lies apparently oblivious to everything else, it has eyes which see everything for miles around, and nothing is permitted to escape its watchful vision; you know that while it appears quiet, submissive and innocent, it is prepared to hurl a steel projectile weighing thousands of pounds at an enemy many miles away; this and much more you can bring to mind with comparatively no effort whatever. But how did the battleship come to be where it is; how did it come

into existence in the first place? All of this you want to know if you are a careful observer.

2. "Follow the great steel plates back through the foundries, see the thousands of men employed in their production; go still further back, and see the ore as it comes from the mine, see it loaded on barges or cars, see it melted and properly treated; go back still further and see the architect and engineers who planned the vessel; let the thought carry you back still further in order to determine why they planned the vessel; you will see that you are now so far back that the vessel is something intangible, it no longer exists, it is now only a thought existing in the brain of the architect; but from where did the order come to plan the vessel? Probably from the Secretary of Defense; but probably this vessel was planned long before the ware was thought of, and that Congress had to pass a bill appropriating the money; possibly there was opposition, and the speeches for or against the bill. Whom do these Congressmen represent? They represent you and me, so that our line of thought begins with the Battleship and ends with ourselves, and we find in the last analysis that our own thought is responsible for this and many other things, of which we seldom think, and a little further reflection will develop the most important fact of all and that is, if someone had not discovered the law by which this tremendous mass of steel and iron could be made to float upon the water, instead of immediately going to the bottom, the battleship could not have come into existence at all.

3. "The law is that, 'the specific gravity of any substance is the weight of any volume of it, compared with an equal volume of water.' The discovery of this law revolutionized every kind of ocean travel, commerce and warfare, and made the existence of the battleship, aircraft carriers, and cruise ships possible."

Day 9 - ACTION:

Putting plans into effect will achieve one's vision.

> *"The self is not something ready-made,*
> *but something in continuous formation*
> *through choice of action."*
> *- John Dewey*

Why daydreams are so disregarded is the simple fact that they are usually never planned out for actualization, no action is taken on them.

You have now learned to think positively and creatively to expand your vision. The next step is to work out how to achieve it, what steps you want to take to bring this about and start doing something in that direction. A person can dream about becoming a famous artist all she wants – but until she puts a pencil, pen or brush to paper and starts cranking out some artwork that can be sold, she will never be able to have any famous works hung in rich patrons' homes. "A long journey is finally accomplished by first taking a single step."

This might be too simple, even common sense, but I've never said that these keys to success were anything other than laws or rules which already existed. What has been presented here is hopefully a common sense explanation and a logical process of thought which outline a workable system of self-help, which anyone can apply and use to improve their lives. These laws have existed so long their source can't even be pointed out in time. Plato and Aristotle have run into these; religious scriptures of all types cover these points. This book translates and compiles these into simple modern Western views so you can take advantage of them.

So, in order to achieve anything, you have to do something about it – not just think good thoughts. Nothing new here, or is there? This is, as I've said, the difference between having dreams and accomplishing them, the difference between architectural drawings and the physical buildings existing as a result. One has to act to acquire, achieve or have anything. You can again see the logic showing up here: to have you must do; to do, you must be; to effectively be, you must think. But if thinking doesn't result in doing something, then nothing will ever be achieved.

Napoleon Hill covered this in some detail in his book:

>   *"The event chosen for this illustration dates back to 1900, when the United States Steel Corporation was being formed. As you read the story, keep in mind these fundamental facts and you will understand how IDEAS have been converted into huge fortunes.*

"First, the huge United States Steel Corporation was born in the mind of Charles M. Schwab, in the form of an IDEA he created through his IMAGINATION!

"Second, he mixed FAITH with his IDEA.

"Third, he formulated a PLAN for the transformation of his IDEA into physical and financial reality.

"Fourth, he put his plan into action with (a) speech at the University Club.

"Fifth, he applied, and followed-through on his PLAN with PERSISTANCE, and backed it with firm DECISION until it had been fully carried out.

"Sixth, he prepared his way for success by a BURNING DESIRE for success.

"THERE ARE NO LIMITATIONS TO THE MIND EXCEPT THOSE WE ACKNOWLEGE.

"BOTH POVERTY AND RICHES ARE THE OFFSPRING OF THOUGHT".

Planning is a key point, one that follows your vision. There's an old adage, a version of which is attributed to Western author Louis Lamour, "Plan your work, work your plan – and always carry a spare".

Part of action is to be personally efficient in what you are doing. Several authors (Covey, Hill, Wattles) mention this point specifically. You can also see that this would be an outgrowth, or logical procession from both a positive outlook, and application of the Golden Rule. One would want to achieve the highest potential possible personally, and as well would want others around him to be efficient and productive when they worked.

Another part of action is to work within your physical limits. While you can exercise to increase your stamina and energy level, don't over-work. This has negative effects mentally and so can slow you down. Pace yourself and work within what you can physically do. This will pay off. Dr. Peale relates one award-winning rowing team was created by being told the secret of winning was to "row slowly." By keeping to the rhythm of the pace, they could pass other anxious, over-energetic teams which had to stop rowing during the race to get everyone back together and in sync. Many activities at work and play have their rhythm. By learning to work within this rhythm, much more work can be achieved for longer periods than "throwing yourself at it."

Part of the plan might be achieving an education or training in a new area which you need to master. Reading this book, or any of the others listed, is a form of education. Modern schooling has this common complaint, "I studied their books and took their tests, passed them all, but didn't learn anything." This problem is because schools have long had the habit of being a brain-dump, where facts and agendas are swallowed wholesale by students to be regurgitated at will, however the students were never enabled with the understanding and practical discipline of being able to organize this data and use that knowledge after they acquire it. You may need to attend school or college to get some of the data you need, but Hill explained it this way, defining the word "educate":

> *"That word is derived from the Latin word 'educo,' meaning to educe, to draw out, to DEVELOP FROM WITHIN. An educated man is not, necessarily, one who has an abundance of general or specialized knowledge. An educated man is one who has so developed the faculties of his mind that he may acquire anything he wants, or its equivalent, without violating the rights of others."*

But the key is action. Set your vision, work out the plan that would achieve it and then implement this plan – starting with something today, right now – that you can do which would start achieving that vision. Don't procrastinate. Take your plan and work out when you want to achieve it, work out then by time period (years, months or even weekly) what has to be achieved by when. Then work from this master list of what you need to accomplish today and by what hour you want to get each sub-step done. Even if you simply say that you are going to have to buy that lottery ticket on the way home from work.

But if you never buy that ticket, you can't win that lottery. So if that is your vision, plan it out and do it.

Day 9 – Exercise:

Try this –

This exercise is from Chapter two of Napoleon Hill's book. While it has to do with achieving wealth, it could as easily be applied to regaining health, achieving happiness or any other possible self-improvement (again, there is far more detail in his book, which is key to achieving financial wealth):

"The method by which DESIRE for riches can be transmuted into its financial equivalent, consists of six definite, practical steps, vis:

"**First**, Fix in your mind the exact amount of money you desire. It is not sufficient merely to say, 'I want plenty of money.'

"**Second**. Determine exactly what you intend to give in return for the money you desire. (There is no such reality as 'something for nothing'.)

"**Third**. Establish a definite date when you intend to possess the money you desire.

"**Fourth**. Create a definite plan for carrying out your desire, and begin at once, whether you are ready or not, to put this plan into action.

"**Fifth**. Write out a clear, concise statement of the amount of money you intend to acquire, name the time limit for its acquisition, state what you intend to give in return for the money, and describe clearly the plan through which you intend to accumulate it.

"**Sixth**. Read your written statement aloud, twice daily, once just before retiring at night, and once after arising in the morning. AS YOU READ – SEE AND FEEL AND BELIEVE YOURSELF AS ALREADY IN POSSESSION OF THE MONEY."

Day 10 - FAITH:

Faith is self-generated, self-created.

"Question: Why are we Masters of our Fate,
the captains of our souls?
Because we have the power to control our thoughts, our attitudes.
That is why many people live in the withering negative world.
That is why many people live in the Positive Faith world.
And you don't have to be a poet or a philosopher
to know which is best."
- Alfred A. Montapert

"Every tomorrow has two handles.
We can take hold of it by the handle of anxiety,
or by the handle of faith."
(author unknown)

Everything in this universe is based on faith. Even scientists, who are strictly trained in observing things only as they exist, depend upon their faith that the laws and facts that they find today will be there tomorrow and forever after that, something which cannot be proved by any test and must be taken on faith. There is some assumption that such observed phenomenon are true or factual – this assumption is faith.

Faith is self-generated. It isn't a quantity that you can pour out of a container or measure with a spoon. It is completely variable from person to person, from subject to subject within each person. Faith depends on creating a belief in something. While a key point in religion, it isn't only relegated to that use. Self-confidence is faith in oneself. Trust is a form of faith in another. But just as someone else can't change your mind for you, so you can't give your faith to someone else. They must generate it for themselves.

What does this have to do with self-help, self-improvement? In Mr. Hill's example of Charles Schwab and US Steel from Day 9, he mentioned the mixture of faith with his idea in order to generate the plan which he then executed. Faith was a second factor to the idea itself. Part of creating a new environment around you will depend on how much self-confidence you have, how much you can trust yourself. This is not a chicken-and-egg conundrum. Faith is simply generated, much like electrical generators create electricity. If you need more faith to make your dreams come to fruition, then simply create more.

While this seems more complex, or more difficult, Dr. Peale covers many examples of utilizing religious faith to handle worry, barriers, lack of energy, lack of happiness and many other common ailments to this society. He has chapters devoted to examples and methods for handling each of the above ailments and more. His book is a good read on this subject.

How to create faith is simple. Dr. Peale quotes William James who said,

> *"The greatest discovery of my generation is that human beings can alter their lives by altering their attitudes of mind."*

This relates: if you need more faith, simply consider that you have more. Find something about whatever bothers you that you can have faith in: the object is the same color from day to day; "you can always count on him to . . . . " Just start thinking down the line of having more faith and more shows up. Consider that you have faith, act like you do, and you soon will be overflowing with it.

All that we have studied through this book brings you up against this next point: By changing your thoughts to creative, positive ones and by changing your attitudes, by creating a vision of what you want to accomplish – you've been creating faith all along, even if starting only with the idea from starting this book that something could be improved – that alone took a great deal of self-generated faith.

For faith is an idea. It isn't tangible, it can't be spent. But it can be invested and get a substantial return. Invest your faith in your vision. The more you put in, the stronger your vision will seem, the more real, and the faster it will accrue for you.

The point of positive thought is that is only works to the exact degree a person commits himself to it. The point of any failure of self-help or self-improvement is the failure to commit. Those who are bad-mouthing some of these books are the one's who will never profit from them, since they cannot invest anything of themselves into it. Some won't even go so far as to read a book on the subject. It's long been said that you can't change anyone else's mind for them. You can, however, set a personal example which others can evaluate their own life against. They can then generate their own faith in the possibility of improving something in their own life.

James Allen put it simply, "The higher he lifts his thoughts, the greater will be his success, the more blessed and enduring will be his achievements."

Charles F. Haanel said it this way, "In order to secure the larger supply your demand must be increased, and as you consciously increase the demand the supply will follow, you will find yourself coming into a larger and larger supply of life, energy and vitality."

Hill points out in some detail that one's faith is a habit. Changing the amount of faith one has is determined by auto-suggestion, what one constantly tells oneself. Simply practicing affirming the vision and result as having already occurred brings forward a strength of faith possibly never seen before. There is a simple mental discipline to building faith. Create the attitude, practice it

- and then it becomes part of you.

Faith follows the laws of thought, just like any attitude – if you need it, create it. Put some faith in your vision, your plan, yourself. And then put on some more for good measure. The more you put in, the more you'll get out.

Day 10 – Exercises:

Try this –

1. Sitting in your chair, consider some times when your trust was betrayed. In each time, go through the sequence of events and determine what action took place which you used to change your trust value. Now go through a number of people or groups in which you have trust currently. Review your association with them and see if you can find the events which increased your trust with them. With these two sets of events, see if you can spot where you changed your level of faith in these individuals or groups and the point that you made that decision.

2. From Haanel: ". . . Concentrate upon your power to create; seek insight, perception; try to find a logical basis for the faith which is in you. Let the thought dwell on the fact that the physical man lives and moves and has his being in the sustainer of all organic life, air, and that he must breathe to live. Then let the thought rest on the fact that the spiritual man also lives and moves and has his being in a similar by subtler energy upon which he must depend for life, and that as in the physical world no life assumes form until after a seed is sown, and no higher fruit than that of parent stock can be produced; so in the spiritual world no effect can be produced until the seed is sown and the fruit will depend upon the nature of the seed, so that the results which you secure depend upon your perception of law in the mighty domain of causation, the highest level of human consciousness. "

3. Take your vision and work it over with faith. Look it over carefully and get the end product in mind. Create the idea and hold it firmly that this has already happened. Consider the specific color, height, consistency, texture, fragrance – all the specifics of the actual thing you want to change. Visualize these in front of you, as solid as you can. Keep at it for 10 or 15 minutes. Again, you can come back and do this later to get better at it.

Day 11 - AFFIRMATION:

Affirmations can be used to strengthen faith and achieve your vision.

"Affirmations are like prescriptions for certain aspects of yourself you want to change".
- Jerry Frankhauser

Words can be powerful tools. This has been recognized and repeated throughout history.

Dr. Peale tells it this way in his book:

"The words we speak have a direct and definite effect upon our thoughts. Thoughts create words, for words are the vehicles of ideas. But words also effect thoughts and help to condition if not to create attitudes. In fact, what often passes for thinking starts with talk. Therefore if the average conversation is scrutinized and disciplined to be sure that it contains peaceful expressions, the result will be peaceful ideas and ultimately, therefore, a peaceful mind."

Affirmations are short-hand statements of your vision. They contain the key point or points that remind you of your whole mental picture you are striving to achieve. These have been given some rough treatment lately, as we went over in Day 7, some have been trying to sing the words without knowing the tune. People can't just idly say they are rich, famous or "improving day after day in every way" unless they have a specific vision, faith and action to back it up. As well, affirmations seem to fail because they are too general. If you are going to keep an appointment at 3:00pm, then you know where and when you have to be there. People tend to use affirmations to each other daily, even as simple as, the office assistant telling you, "You've got a 3 o'clock meeting today," or your spouse reminding you to bring a pound of hamburger back on your way home.

Affirmations can be far more powerful than the shopping list, though. If you plan out exactly what you have to do to get your vision accomplished, having a short version of that vision can jump-start your attitude at the beginning of the day and keep it in front of you the whole day. This is Napoleon Hill's advice to write that statement out and read it to yourself at least two times a day. But note how he said to do it: "AS YOU READ – SEE AND FEEL AND BELIEVE YOURSELF AS ALREADY IN POSSESSION OF THE MONEY."

That is the key point. Unless you commit something to that piece of paper, it will be like all the old newspapers that are swept up in cities across this planet each night by sanitation departments and janitors, only to be dumped in refuse bins. These papers have many more words printed on them, far more artfully and professionally than your little piece of paper. Yet they achieve nothing in and of themselves. Take out a business card. It, too, has words on it. Does it do anything? If you lost it today, would it matter – just get another, eh? But that business card could be read as an affirmation of your current job, something that you are actively creating and achieving. Read with feeling, and belief, you can get quite a surge if you do it in a positive attitude.

Affirmations are a short-hand statement of your vision. Your vision is nothing but a daydream unless you are willing to go full-tilt at it, "firing on all eight cylinders" and ready to set the world on fire to get it. That is the power behind those words. That is all the power behind these words. Just what you put into them, nothing more.

Hill sold over 7 million copies of his book and put this above datum in the second chapter of his book, repeating it several times throughout. He considered it that vital.

Haanel covered it this way:

"Words are thoughts and are therefore an invisible and invincible power which will finally objectify themselves in the form they are given.

"Words may become mental places what will live forever, of they may become shacks which the first breeze will carry away. They may delight the eye as well as the ear, they may contain all knowledge; in them we find the history of the past as well as the hope of the future; they are

living messengers from which every human and superhuman activity is born.

"The beauty of the word consists in the beauty of the thought; the power of the word consists in the power of the thought, and the power of the thought consists in its vitality."

Dr. Covey has more insight into this matter:

"In effective personal leadership, visualization and affirmation techniques emerge naturally out of a foundation of well thought through purposes and principles that become the center of a person's life. They are extremely powerful in re-scripting and re-programming, into writing deeply committed-to purposes and principles into one's heart and mind."

Not all of our self-help authors required affirmations as part of achieving self-improvement. I include it here as an explanation and additional tool which can help you achieve your own improvement in your own life.

Day 11 – Exercise:

Try this –

While Napoleon Hill's book and principles are devoted to achieving prosperity, these can readily be converted to improving any area of your life:

"**First**. Go into some quiet spot (preferably in bed at night) where you will not be disturbed or interrupted, close your eyes, and repeat aloud, (so you may hear your own words) the written statement of the amount of money you intend to accumulate, the time limit for its accumulation, and a description of the service or merchandise you intend to give in return for the money. As you carry out these instructions, SEE YOURSELF ALREADY IN POSSESSION OF THE MONEY.

"**Second**. Repeat this program night and morning until you can see, (in your imagination) the money you intend to accumulate.

"**Third**. Place a written copy of your statement where you can see it night and morning, and read it just before retiring, and upon arising until it has been memorized."

Day 12 - POWER THROUGH PRAYER:

Belief in a Supreme Being or Higher Power – tapping into one's relationship with the Supreme Being increases one's own abilities and power.

> *"My religion consists of a humble admiration of the illimitable superior spirit who reveals himself in the slight details we are able to perceive with our frail and feeble mind."*
> *- Albert Einstein*

The vast majority of humans on this planet (one recent survey has it as high as 96% in America) recognize some sort of higher power. Factually, atheists are a very small minority. And many of these are agnostics, meaning that for them, the jury is still out on the matter.

The connection between self-help and this higher power is insisted upon in most self-help books and merely recognized as a given in the rest. Haanel and Wattles call this power by different names and give other technical details about the connection. Dr. Peale is very direct in connecting the benefits of self-help directly with God, giving many, many examples and techniques directly associated with New and Old Testament Scriptures. Al Ghazzali also directly links self-improvement with Allah, quoting different parts of the Koran in doing so. (During this search, I did not find any Buddhist or other religion's bestselling self-improvement books that met the requisites for this study; principally this book was written with Western thought on the matter; in the Appendix, there is a short summary and conclusion about the books used in the original study.)

Undeniably, then, if a person is to get the most out of his own course in self-improvement, one must take God, or the Universal Mind, or any other phrasing, into account. (While there might be a commonality between religions, this is another study and beyond the scope of this book. For our arguments here, and due to the almost identical approach that the authors mentioned have used, we'll consider that they are all talking about the same Entity.) Probably the most interesting point in writing this chapter is that there are so many different opinions about God – probably as many as there are grains of sand or pebbles on the beach – every person has a slightly different one. Without purposely stepping on anyone's toes on this subject, let's boil down what these various authors hold in common in relation to God and self-help:

- This Power is everywhere, omnipresent, permeating all forms and matter; all parts of Creation are a part of the whole, we are all part of this Power

- As such, the Power cannot be subjugated or tricked, etc. This Power plays no favorites, makes no exceptions, is not subject to petition or sympathy ploys.

- This Power has a continuing purpose of creating forms and is the source of all supply.

- This Power deals in abundance through all its forms; this concept enables all such creations to have abundance in their own lives.

- It is through creative imagination that one is linked to this Power, which is the source of intuition, hunches, genius and inspiration.

- A person's cooperation with this Power determines one's success.

- Only through a feeling of gratitude will such a cooperative connection be possible.

- Tapping into this power is only possible through a creative, harmonious, non-competitive basis. One will receive only as one gives; what one receives will make it more possible to give.

The various religious texts and scriptures contain words which describe the above relationships and rules regarding our relationship with God, by any name. Dr. Peale, whose book is written entirely from a religious view of self-help, gives innumerable examples of people being able to use the Bible to improve their lives. And innumerable is no understatement. For every story in his book, I'm sure there are a hundred or a thousand more.

Dr. Peale also relates:

> *"Prayer power is a manifestation of energy. Just as there exist scientific techniques for the release of atomic energy, so there are scientific procedures for the release of spiritual energy through the mechanism of prayer."*

Consider this logically: we can approach, contact and receive gifts from an omnipresent, omnipotent source. We only have to do this in a specific manner to achieve consistent results. This seems more science than religion.

Indeed, Dr. Peale relates a story where two industrialists, perplexed by a problem, decided to pray for a solution, given the formula, "Where two or three are gathered together in my name, there am I in the midst of them." (Matthew 18:20). Since this didn't get the expected results, they consulted a local preacher who pointed out additional formulaic phrases, namely, "According to your faith, be it unto you." (Matthew 9:29), and "What things soever ye desire, when ye pray, believe that ye receive them, and ye shall have them." (Mark 11:24). These three prayed accordingly. After several such thorough sessions of prayer, these three all affirmed that their prayers had been answered. Investigation of the results showed that the results were satisfactory and according to their prayers.

We have, then, a precise scientific approach to improving any aspect of one's life. Part of this approach is the recognition of this Power according to the observed and tested rules these various authors have researched and written down for us.

A part of this procedure is prayer, as mentioned above. Now, all these authors do not agree upon any set formula or procedure for prayer. Dr. Peale covers a wide variety of forms that he and others use. What is common between them is that there is an open communication between the person and this Power. Haanel suggests sitting quietly, relaxed and simply opening one's thoughts to this Power, sending one's visualization and desire. Wattles adds that one must be then thankful for having received that gift, continuing along the line that one always acknowledges the receipt of anything requested in the past tense. Even the word "Amen," according to the International Standard Bible Encyclopedia, "is generally used as an adverb of assent or confirmation--fiat, 'so let it be.'"

One of the more interesting points regarding prayer aligns with earlier points we've covered. Were one to completely eradicate non-positive thoughts from one's mind and as well adopt an ethical/moral code to keep this in place constantly in life, one could fall under the description of "living your prayer." Actually, this is a phrase in the New Testament, "Be always joyful; pray continually; give thanks whatever happens; for this is what God in Christ wills for you." (1 Thessalonians 5:16-18). Were a person to achieve this level of thought and action, according to the principles we have covered so far in this book, nothing would be impossible to achieve or acquire; all of his/her relationships would be as rewarding as he/she wished.

While this is a book of Western ideas of self-help, and so any discussion of God would bring references to the Judeo-Christian approaches, study of Al Ghazzali's The Alchemy of Happiness shows definite parallels. Though beyond the scope of this book, but given that such writings have continued through the thousands of years the Bible was written and into our current times, it is probable that the principles outlined here are universal in application, regardless of form of religion.

Day 12 – Exercises:

Try this –

From Dr. Peale's book:

1. "The formula is (1) PRAYERIZE, (2) PICTURIZE, (3) ACTUALIZE. " . . .

2. "To assure something worth while happening, first pray about it and test it according to God's will; then print a picture of it on your mind as happening, holding the picture firmly in consciousness. Continue to surrender the picture to God's will – that is to say, put the matter in God's hands – and follow God's guidance. Work hard and intelligently, thus doing your part to hold the picturization firmly in your thoughts. Do this and you will be astonished at the strange ways in which the picturization comes to pass. In this manner the picture "actualizes. " That which you have "prayerized" and "picturized" "actualizes" according to the pattern of your basic realizable wish when conditioned by invoking God's power upon it, and if, moreover, you give fully of yourself to its realization."

Dr. Robert C. Worstell

Day 13 - PEACE:

Peace of Mind is attainable through self-control.

"He who is of calm and happy nature
will hardly feel the pressure of age,
but to him who is of an opposite disposition
youth and age are equally a burden."
- Plato

Peace of Mind is available to anyone, at any time.

Practically, we've already gone over how to achieve this. Per Haanel, this is simply regaining control over one's own thoughts, as we covered in the beginning chapters of this book. These were the beginning exercises of sitting in a quiet space and relaxing, gaining control over your thoughts. Any skill must be exercised in order to become reasonably adept at it, and so the reason to invoke the now familiar, "Practice makes perfect. " Relaxing one's physical state and being able to rid all possible, accessible non-positive thoughts is a required step, as well as filling it with positive thoughts.

More vital in all these is the ability to simply reach a "silence" or "quietude" internally so that intuition and insight are more readily accessible. It is through these creative thoughts and connections and interchange that all sort of possible improvements can be achieved for our human race.

James Allen put it most eloquently:

"Calmness of mind is one of the beautiful jewels of wisdom. It is the result of long and patient effort in self-control. Its presence is an indication of ripened experience, and of a more than ordinary knowledge of the laws and operations of thought.

"A man becomes calm in the measure that he understands himself as a thought-evolved being. For such knowledge necessitates the understanding of others as the result of thought, and as he develops a right understanding, and sees ever more clearly the internal relations of things by the action of cause and effect, he ceases to fuss, fume, worry, and grieve. He remains poised, steadfast, serene.

"The calm man, having learned how to govern himself, knows how to adapt himself to others. And they, in turn reverence his physical strength. They feel that they can learn from him and rely upon him. The more tranquil a man becomes, the greater is his success, his influence, his power for good. Even the ordinary trader will find his business prosperity increase as he develops a greater self-control and equanimity, for people will always prefer to deal with a man whose demeanor is equitable. . . .

> "How many people do we know who sour their lives, who ruin all that is sweet and beautiful by explosive tempers, who destroy their poise of character and make bad blood! Only the wise man, only he whose thoughts are controlled and purified, makes the winds and the storms of the soul obey him.

> "Tempest-tossed souls, wherever you may be, under whatever conditions you may live, know this: In the ocean of life the isles of blessedness are smiling and the sunny shore of your ideal awaits your coming. Keep your hands firmly upon the helm of thought. In the core of your soul reclines the commanding Master; He does but sleep; wake Him. Self-control is strength. Right thought is mastery. Calmness is power. Say unto your heart, 'Peace, Be Still.' "

And that is the simplicity of peace of mind. Achieve a mental quiet through practice. Then all measure of things are possible, per these texts. Those who cast about for amusement, who plug their ears with loud music, who play the TV incessantly when alone or with family – these are seeking to avoid something, to not face or confront some idea or thought or mental noise that constantly distracts, depresses, angers or intimidates them.

Yet all thought is created. Humankind has simply not been able to routinely enable people to learn to sit quietly and sort these thoughts out, to bring them under control. Rural societies have the advantage of large spaces between themselves and other areas, even other families. So there are long spaces of quiet which must be endured. While now we can fill this void with satellite radio, DVD players and whatnot, perhaps we shouldn't. One friend of mind, a full generation younger, was aghast that I would simply turn off the radio when there was nothing valuable to listen to, that I would use the time driving between rural towns simply completing thoughts to logical conclusions. But he was raised on video games – I grew up in an age where the early computers ran on tape and punch cards.

My parents can remember plowing and cultivating behind mules, the times when tractors first became popular in farming. Those were truly quiet days for thoughtful people. Yet the trade-off is in these days of high percentage disposable income. We now have the time to think, to philosophize – which for the Founders of this country and historically before that, was the sovereign territory of the rich. Benjamin Franklin, for one, retired at age 40. With few exceptions, those who could put their thoughts in order and take the time to write them down for others had already made their success.

These days, however, one can take a period of time, look up the great masters on the Internet as public domain or order printed books and get them delivered in days from booksellers on this same Internet system. If one can afford the time (and paper to print them off or hard-drive space to store them on), he can have any amount of classic works at his fingertips or as digital recordings.

So it is up to us to do the research and publish our conclusions. It is up to us to find those who have been down these roads before, to stand on the shoulders of these giants to see further, per Isaac Newton, and describe what we see.

The steps I've compiled in this short book show simple steps that anyone can take, an introduction to a very potent subject.

This book makes it possible for anyone to achieve peace of mind and a peaceful existence. One need only read and try, then, through demonstrating its usefulness and application for oneself, create the faith needed to practice and continue improving one's own conditions.

Day 13 – Exercise:

Try this –

Dr. Peale received these instructions from the ace pilot Eddie Rickenbacker, who developed an unflappable calm which served him well in life in all sorts of circumstances:

1. "First, collapse physically. Practice this several times a day. Let go every muscle in the body. Conceive of yourself as a jellyfish, getting your body into complete looseness. Form a mental picture of a huge burlap bag of potatoes. Then mentally cut the bag, allowing the potatoes to roll out. What is more relaxed than a burlap bag?

2. "The second element in the formula is to "drain the mind." Several times each day drain the mind of all irritation, all resentment, disappointment, frustration, and annoyance. Unless you drain the mind frequently and regularly, these unhappy thoughts will accumulate until a major blasting-out process will be necessary. Keep the mind drained of all factors which would impede the flow of relaxed power.

3. "Third, think spiritually. To think spiritually means to turn the mind at regular intervals to God. At least three times a day 'lift up your eyes unto the hills. ' This keeps you in tune with God's harmony. It refills you with peace."

Day 14 - MASTER MIND:

Surround yourself with people around you who think as you do.

The composite mind will achieve the composite vision shared.

"Never doubt that a small group of thoughtful committed people can change the world: indeed it's the only thing that ever has!"
-Margaret Meade

The "Master Mind" is having a group of people that you support and owe your support to. It is also your use of the earlier principles listed, in order to create that support, both to and from you.

This concept is the reason for churches and their purpose. The faith you create, if shared, can accomplish far more with a group pushing it than the same number of persons pushing that purpose individually.

The same principle works for corporations. Dr. Covey goes over this in his analysis of getting companies to do realistic mission statements. These are realistic in that they involve everyone from the top manager to the "lowliest" employee (if there is such a thing in actuality.) He describes a hotel chain he visited to train their employees. Through various incidents he observed personally, he saw that they had a unique and personal view of service to their customers. Employees would drop whatever they were doing and help the person in front of them, making sure that the customer had whatever he wanted. This wasn't just the bell boy or the steward, but he mentions seeing a window washer come down from his high vantage to help a woman with a walker get into the lobby safely and easily, then return to his window washing. When he asked the manager what his secret was, he pulled out the mission statement. Not just the organization's mission statement, but also then pulled out that particular hotel's mission statement, a version of the first, but developed for that particular hotel. He explained that the hotel staff as a whole had developed it. Further, he pulled out several mission statements, which would go down into departments and sub-departments – each developed by the persons in that area in their own words, each a specialized version of the overall statement. This hotel team built itself and had extraordinarily valuable service as a result, an asset which cannot be bought and installed or repaired, but which must be grown. (Again, get his book. It is extremely well written and sensible.)

A group doesn't just have a purpose, but lives it, grows it. When you see some small country church which is losing its membership, you can see that they could improve on their faith and their vision to attract more parishioners. Similarly, companies that have high turnover problems have probably never truly built a team and do not share a common purpose nor do they truly agree about how to go about getting it.

Go Thunk Yourself!

This applies to self-help in that a person won't get as far on his own as one can with another or several persons having the same dream or vision. Many artists, like Thomas Hart Benton and Charley Russell had wives who were the actual behind-the-scene business partner, making sure they got top dollar for their art, managing the household economics and also the social event calendar to ensure the marketing, sales, delivery and PR functions were covered. A two-person team with one vision.

Larger than that, corporations have been formed based entirely on a single vision. Napoleon Hill tells in his book that Carnegie didn't have to know all there was about steel-making, he had fifty people he trusted to make those day-to-day decisions in running his business. Ray Kroc counted on his managers and franchise owners to deliver superior service to their customers – after he trained them in his "Hamburger U" in the basement of one of his Midwestern franchises. Mr. Kroc made millionaires out of bun, packaging and condiment suppliers because he trusted them to supply his business and kept sending them orders due to that trust; as his business grew, so did theirs. Mr. Kroc supplied the vision, they got on board and pushed this vision. They shared Kroc's faith and became millionaires as a result.

Fully half of Dr. Covey's book covers the finer points of building an effective team. The reasons for doing so are also covered in Hill's book, in addition to Haanel's. One can have a personal vision. But sharing this vision, giving others something to have faith in and push with their own coordinated actions can make the dream far bigger, far more expansive than a single individual could ever attempt on his own. The physical universe reality follows the vision. When the vision is expanded by additional people adding to it, the resulting reality is larger by multiples, as the power increases by factors, not just addition.

Conversely, where a company isn't expanding or running into repeated difficulties, it has gone off purpose (if it ever had truly defined it originally) and the vision shared by the founder is not being participated in by the lower echelon managers and staff. This single datum is covered over and over in various business texts far beyond the scope of this single book. Here we just see that the principles described in this book are basic, fundamental laws of operation for an individual and extend up to the largest corporations and governments.

So, build your team, share your vision, generate trust in each other; there are no limits to expansion providing you follow these fundamental laws we've laid out here.

Day 14 – Exercises:

Try this –

1. Take your vision statement and work out how big it factually needs to be to accomplish what you want to achieve.

2. From this, list out the general functions you will need, in sequence, to achieve this vision.

3. Working backward from how many products you intend to produce, sell and deliver, figure out how many people you might need to help you, based on how many of these functions can be handled by a single person or how many persons might be needed for each function (like warehousing and distribution, for instance.) The following steps make this simpler:

4. Take a big piece of paper. Write the vision/mission statement at the top.

5. Write out the functions to achieve this vision in a sequence, each function having a separate spot starting from one side and going to the other.

6. Put a name for each job, depending on how many functions each job holds or vice-versa.

7. Now write a short mission statement for each post of how this job/function relates to the overall vision/mission statement and helps accomplish it

8. Review the whole thing and adjust it until you are happy with it.

9. Now you are ready to form your "Master Mind" by finding people (or they will find you) to help you attain this vision.

Summary:

Why this stuff is important.

This book concerns everyone. Essentially, it says that there is a workable system for self-improvement which has been tested and proved through popular subscription – people like it and buy its authors' works. If one believes the data from these books to be true, then all manner of improvement in life is open to that person.

But let me quote this value as seen by the authors themselves:

"The operation of this thought process is seen in those fortunate natures that possess everything that others must acquire by toil, who never have a struggle with conscience because they always act correctly, can never conduct themselves otherwise than with tact, learn everything easily, complete everything they begin with a happy knack, live in eternal harmony with themselves, without every reflecting much what they do, or ever experiencing difficulty or toil.

"The fruit of this thought is, as it were, a gift of the gods, but a gift which few as yet realize, appreciate, or understand. The recognition of the marvelous power which is possessed by the mind under proper conditions and the fact that this power can be utilized, directed, and made available for the solution of every human problem is of transcendental importance. "

 Thomas F. Haanel, <u>The Master Key System</u>

and:

 "The real battle of life is one of ideas; it is being fought out by the few against the many; on the one side is the constructive and creative thought, on the other side the destructive or negative thought; the creative thought is dominated by an ideal, the passive thought is dominated by appearances. On both sides are men of science, men of letters, and men of affairs." (ibid.)

 "All that a man achieves and all that he fails to achieve is the direct result of his own thoughts. In a justly ordered universe, where loss of equipoise would mean total destruction, individual responsibility must be absolute. A man's weakness and strength, purity and impurity, are his own and not another man's. They are brought about by himself and not by another; and they can only be altered by himself, never by another. His condition is also his own, and not another man's. His sufferings and his happiness are evolved from within. As he thinks, so is he; as he continues to think, so he remains.

 "A strong man cannot help a weaker unless that weaker is willing to be helped. And even then the weak man must become strong of himself. He must, by his own efforts, develop the strength which he admires in another. None but himself can alter his condition."

James Allen, <u>As A Man Thinketh</u>.

and:

"The dreamers are the saviors of the world. As the visible world is sustained by the invisible, so men, through all their trials and sins and sordid vocations, are nourished by the beautiful visions of their solitary dreamers. Humanity cannot forget its dreamers; it cannot let their ideals fade and die; it lives in them; it knows them as the realities which it shall one day see and know. Composer, sculptor, painter, poet, prophet, sage--these are the makers of the after-world, the architects of heaven. The world is beautiful because they have lived. Without them, laboring humanity would perish. He who cherishes a beautiful vision, a lofty ideal in his heart, will one day realize it. Columbus cherished a vision of another world and he discovered it. Copernicus fostered the vision of a multiplicity of worlds and a wider universe, and he revealed it. Buddha beheld the vision of a spiritual world of stainless beauty and perfect peace, and he entered into it.

"Cherish your visions; cherish your ideals. Cherish the music that stirs in your heart, the beauty that forms in your mind, the loveliness that drapes your purest thoughts. For out of them will grow all delightful conditions, all heavenly environment; of these, if you but remain true to them, your world will at last be built.

"To desire is to obtain; to aspire is to achieve. Shall man's basest desires receive the fullest measure of gratification, and his purest aspirations starve for lack of sustenance? Such is not the Law. Such a condition can never obtain: 'Ask and receive.'

"Dream lofty dreams, and as you dream, so shall you become. Your vision is the promise of what you shall one day be; your ideal is the prophecy of what you shall at last unveil.

"The greatest achievement was at first and for a time a dream. The oak sleeps in the acorn; the bird waits in the egg. And in the highest vision of a soul a waking angel stirs. Dreams are the seedlings of realities." (ibid.)

"The world in which you live is not primarily determined by outward conditions and circumstances but by thoughts that habitually occupy your mind. Remember the wise words of Marcus Aurelius, one of the great thinkers of antiquity, who said, 'A man's life is what his thoughts make of it.'

"It has been said that the wisest man who ever lived in America was Ralph Waldo Emerson, the Sage of Concord. Emerson declared, 'A man is what he thinks about all day long.'

Go Thunk Yourself!

"A famous psychologist says, 'There is a deep tendency in human nature to become precisely like that which you habitually imagine yourself to be.'

"It has been said that thoughts are things, that they actually possess dynamic power. Judged by the power they exercise one can readily accept such an appraisal. You can actually think yourself into or out of situations. You can make yourself ill with your thoughts and by the same token you can make yourself well by the use of a different and healing type of thought. Think one way and you attract the conditions which that type of thinking indicates. Think another way and you can create an entirely different set of conditions. Conditions are created by thoughts far more powerfully than conditions create thoughts."

- Norman Vincent Peale, <u>The Power of Positive Thinking</u>.

I give you here concrete principles which you can use to improve your life in any aspect or on the whole. You can test these as much as you want, they belong to no author as his sacrosanct copyright; they were observed by Plato and Aristotle and many thinkers since. That this Western world has isolated a few of these as important enough to re-publish, re-sell and re-distribute long after their authors have returned to dust is the highest validation of them as basic and true, useful principles for self-improvement.

There are perhaps no factual limits to what can be accomplished in using these principles. Logically, one could see that there are no real barriers to thought and imagination, so conceivably no limit to what could be accomplished in the physical universe.

Even while Haanel above points out that one cannot change another for him, while Wattles warns not to get into occult practices in an effort to change another against their will, Peale also tells us a story where a woman restored her marriage and avoided divorce through the above principles, Covey tells of deciding to handle a disruptive conflict he was having for months with an associate – only to find that the associate wanted to handle it as well. One doesn't know what another wants particularly, but by the tools above – visualization, faith, prayer, action – many, many intersocial and intercultural affairs can be resolved. One doesn't know that the other doesn't want to change or improve – your work would minimally give them that chance.

Several of the authors (Haanel, Peale, Wattles) say to think and visualize as big as you can, that these make the smaller problems fall away as insignificant. With the application of the principle involved in the "Master Mind," a wide association of individuals with the common ideal will achieve many, widespread – even global effects. One such example is the view of Human Rights, which started with Locke, Jefferson and the Founding Fathers, then was spread through the globe due to the efforts of the United States UN delegate, Eleanor Roosevelt, who drafted and got agreement from other delegates enough to sign it into a UN resolution – all from her New York apartment. Now this is a held standard across the globe, defended and advanced with economic sanctions to those spineless dicto-crats who insist on violating it. One by one, these countries are being forced to accede to this thought, this vision which is shared now by so many internationally.

It is my personal hope that within our own lifetimes we might see world peace. Certainly if the principles that these authors and their reading public found so useful were spread across this globe, the planet and its culture would be a more positive, less strife-driven place. Peace would then be possible, with a decent standard of living and defended liberties for every single member of humankind. But it is up to you and I to carry this torch and to forward these ideals and bring them to real substance.

That is why this stuff is important.

Appendix A:

The books that made up this study and why you should read them.

One might think it odd that an author would suggest that someone to stop reading his book and go out to buy and read another instead. But that is the exact premise of this book. Many philosophers have covered these points throughout history. Much of this data has been lost and then recovered and republished in different form, even different languages. The authors I've quoted in this book are far more experienced than I, more widely read and these books often represent the acme of their success as an author.

This study was initially made up of best selling self-help classics who continued to sell and be distributed widely(for free in many cases) after the author's death. This gave us three key acid-tests:

1. The text was found appealing to its audience and purchased widely.

2. The text is continuing to be found as useful, regardless of grammar, language or style changes.

3\. The sales of the book didn't depend on the personal charisma of the author or social fads and whims.

These requisites produced books which gave a body of data consistently found useful and workable by their readers. That was the premise of the study: there were possibly common datums in use throughout self-help texts that could lead to a single common philosophy or even science of self-improvement – something that anyone could apply and use, since these were then probably based on naturally occurring phenomenon or laws.

Once the bulk of the research was done, more recent books were compared to see if these data were being used in present time, which would explain current best-seller status, since they used workable principles. One was selected based on its all-time record-setting tape sales and continuing high sales years after it was originally published. It was found to have the same data as the older texts and so contributed proof to the study's premise.

This is not an exhaustive study of all possible self-help books or tapes. The subject of weight-loss was left alone, as well as many religious tracts and "occult" publications. However, the principles uncovered actually started explaining how some books were continuing best-sellers and others hit discount bins and clearance racks almost immediately after publication. As well, it explained how some works continued to be passed around on the Internet and republished even a century or more after the author died.

This particular book was written in the style and method of many modern computer books: "Learn _____ in X days/hours." While this isn't particularly true (it factually takes years to get really professional at something), it does place introductory data into the hands of people who are currently pushed for time. This format doesn't give a person other than that introduction to the subject, so that he/she can then continue study on their own.

This is why I tell people to read the other books. They are the best work to study for that part of the whole body of self-improvement principles.

For instance,

- If you want to get wealthy, study Hill or Wattles.
- If your self-improvement is of a religious bent, study Peale.
- The best book to build a personal and business ethic is Covey.
- For the scientific, technical details of how self-help works, study Haanel.
- An overview and key explanation is found in Allen.
- In getting along with people, Carnegie is the best overall.

- For improving your outlook in life and general happiness, consult Carnegie and Peale.

These books overlap and cover different points in their own styles. That is the use of this book – to show you when and where to bridge off when certain personal points need attention. But I would recommend you study all these books in order to get a real conceptual understanding of all the principles outlined here.

This book I've written doesn't cover every single detail or the scientific theory and proved facts behind these 14 points. I've only taken the most common points and presented them in a style which is readable and easily digestible for our modern hectically-paced existence.

And I am not saying at any point that I am any past master of these points presented; I have my own row to hoe. This book is no perfect example of anything. At points, I've been perhaps too critical of certain institutions in society who could stand a great deal of improvement. I only point out in this book what I have found in a simple style which can be easily digested and hopefully used as a springboard for other study and self-improvement by the reader.

That is why I tell you: Buy and read the other books – make this a professional study. Prove these points to yourself, don't just accept my study as Law. Better yet, write your own book using these principles applied to your own area of expertise.

Dr. Robert C. Worstell

Appendix B:

Brief history and apparent origin of American self-help

These books have common threads. The latest, Covey's 7 Habits (1989), was based on study of 200 years of self-help texts in America. In the 20th century we have Peale's Positive Thinking (1952), preceded by Hill's Think and Grow Rich (1937) and Dale Carnegie's How to Win Friends (1937). Ten years earlier is James Allen's As A Man Thinketh (1923). Another decade prior were Charles F. Haanel's Master Key System (1912) and Wallace D. Wattles' Science of Getting Rich (1910).

Possible influences on these works can be attributed to the environmental influences of their times. Peale's influence might have been the Cold War mentality of the late 40's and early 50's. Hill, while starting his research twenty years earlier, published during the depression for the stated purpose of getting enabling people to start making money again. As well, this was the publishing time of Dale Carnegie. Allen published after World War I, while Haanel and Wattles published prior, during America's affluence period. While the later works all might be touted as responses to war and recovery, this theory doesn't hold for the earliest works, whose authors had never seen a whole world at war.

A more interesting line of approach is the common principles which have surfaced in the different books. Many of these authors are known to be included under the umbrella of "New Thought." According to a pamphlet put out by the Calgary New Thought Center, Peale is also included as being heavily influenced by New Thought authors. Haanel himself references Judge (Thomas) Troward who lectured and wrote widely on the subject of "Mental Science" from 1902 to his death in 1916. The Calgary pamphlet credits Troward with being one of the two "taproots" of the New Thought movement. Other sources, such as the Santa Rosa Church of Religious Science, traces the history back through Troward to Emerson and Transcendentalism to Kant and then originally to Plato who first coined the term "transcendent."

The other taproot was Phineas P. Quimby, who cured and trained many healers, who in turn were able to train others, forming organizations and churches as they spread. Of interest to this study is that the current form of spiritual treatment for one, the New Thought Church of Religious Science's, that of giving thanks after prayer, which is done in the past tense, that of having already received the object/request prayed for.

New Thought is itself inclusive of a wide-ranging span of thoughts and ideas, ranging from mystic to biblical to scientific and everything in between. It currently has perhaps the greatest collection of modern thinkers and philosophers willing to tackle even the subject of the God directly.

It's not surprising particularly that New Thought ideas would then influence self-help so widely. What is surprising is that this one philosophic school would sprout continuing best sellers and/or be the source for underlying principles of self-improvement.

The conclusion of this study, regardless of the sources of the material, is that there is a simple system of self-improvement/self-help based on principles which are native to nature and can be proved scientifically to be effective where applied exactly.

Appendix C:

How to "de-dupe" someone.

A dupe is a person who has been operating on questionable data as gospel truth. Perhaps you know one who has "sold himself upriver" to some "cult" or oddball quasi-religious sect. Otherwise the person seems sensible enough and in good health. If you wanted to get him/her out of that scene, it could be tricky. "De-programming" was a practice which was based on illegally grabbing and holding someone against their will while someone forcibly re-indoctrinated them.

This didn't work because of the phrase "against their will." The only person who can change a person is the person him/herself.

When a person's beliefs are challenged, he/she sets up all sorts of defenses in action against the attacker. So it is no solution to simply deride or be critical of the person you would like to change. Snide comments only alienate them from you, such that anything you say is considered suspect.

Your tools in this case are application of the principles above: Prayer, Visualization, Action. Treat the person as you would want to be treated – friendliness, honesty, understanding. Understand where the person is coming from, understand the basis of his beliefs. Only then can you spot where that person is accepting illogical data on the basis of faith, only then can you understand how the person is using this belief to prop up his/her life beliefs.

That person has probably a complete set of data and patterned solutions which he/she has been given to deride or de-power the outside world. Much of this data is probably untrue. Asked what these data consist of, with a true aspect of understanding, they will tell you. But when confronted with factual data of how the actual world works – that it isn't really as evil as one was led to believe – such views will shift.

Views are only as solid as the faith behind them. People are constantly re-evaluating data in their lives by comparing existing scenes to those they previously knew/witnessed/read about. People are re-programming themselves all the time – it's called growing older. People learn as they go on living. Non-positive thought can be considered thought which is incomplete in the thought process. Given enough time, one can work out more positive solutions to any problem. And so, old "hatreds" tend to resolve over time, as people find new and better solutions to cope with the problems they confront.

The short-hand of de-duping someone:

1. "Prayerize, Visualize, Actualize"
2. Treat them as you would like to be treated.

3. Understand where they are coming from.
4. Give them your data and help them understand it.

Eventually, given enough time, a person who moves out of such a "cult" environment will adjust and "blend in" with the new environment. If they know the above data and do their own research, they will eventually quit hating that group which they left, despite all the injustices which may have been committed on them (baring actual illegal activities which have their own recourse.)

One key point is that the person must take responsibility for his/her own actions, visualizations and thoughts which led him/her to chose that "cult" to live their life with. With this and active pursuit of real understanding, these people can then start living their lives. It will take some re-education, but will eventually happen regardless.

I give the above steps so that some might make the transition more easily, more quickly. It's been said that it takes some twelve years for a person to transition back to normal life after being in a "cult," particularly if kicked out or forced to leave in self-defense. By doing the above actions, such a time period could be considerably shortened in duration.

Amicable education is the key.

Addendum

There are certain observations and remarks that can be, and should be made regarding self-help and the system discovered as a whole, as well as potential applications of it to broader areas such as society and government.

First, logic says that practically there are no limits to what one can achieve with this system. For as one continues to work, that person will find that there are fewer and fewer limits as he goes, perhaps finding that more of these are grounded in the physical plane than spiritual.

The nature of this system demands one evolve a synergy between the subconscious (per Haanel and others), the conscious spirit/soul which inhabits the body and the Divine. Covey devotes an entire chapter to this concept. "Creative cooperation" he also calls it.

Other studies either tend to confuse the body and the spirit or try to ignore the Divine influence by being "scientific" about it. Practically, more and more scientific studies are beginning to recognize the limits of pure materialistic research, i. e. , denying any causation that cannot occur outside of strictly physical limits. But as well, the role of intuition has been determined to be integral to science's breakthroughs. Intuition requires all three factors of the subconscious,

conscious and Divine minds to operate in cooperation. (Body, Mind, Spirit)

The fourth factor in such a synergy would be purpose. For what reason is the action occurring? What are you trying to accomplish? We deal still with the objective part of this – that of the conscious mind – to determine this purpose, in alignment with the Divine and the limits to the facilities of the subconscious.

One can have all sorts of different purposes, either constructive or non-constructive (destructive), positive or non-positive (negative). I describe these in these terms to show the practical applications. Construct means literally to build together and destruct means to build apart. Both are based on the point of create, one creating cooperatively and the other creating divisively. Earlier in this book, I mentioned that there was only positive and non-positive, that thinking was done based on solutions which were either not thought through or incompletely solved. Non-positive solutions were those which were using partial or incomplete solutions which did not result in optimal results for all concerned. The indicators of these are the negative or "mis-" emotions of antagonism, anger, grief, covert hostility, apathy and so on. Positive emotions include conservative support, enthusiasm, exhilaration and serenity. These last are those which will get the most constructive work done.

Purposes can therefore be determined to be constructive or destructive by what emotions they generate and how much they benefit current societal elements and future ones. The optimal solution would generate tremendous support and solve various problems both in the present and in the future.

The point I am leading up to is that people have this choice: they can use this data to create immensely useful corporate, governmental and religious organizations. Immense talent can be released and employed to create our next masterpieces. Or conversely, this could be used to create terrible criminal organizations and weapons that can destroy this planet or render it unlivable.

The interesting observed safeguard is that those who are creating positive works are dealing with more thought-out, more optimal solutions and so will continue to succeed. Those who are dealing in destructive efforts have built in failures, since their solutions are flawed and incompletely thought out. As well, these organizations do not factually engender the intimate support of their associates. Jealousy, fear and greed are common emotions and attitudes. So such groups are then self-destructive.

This is the point of building non-competitively cooperative organizations. This attitude must be external as well as internal. Any company must realize that this universe we occupy revolves around abundance of supply. Any lack of sufficient food, housing, clothing or any other basic want have all been solvable since at least 1950 for the entire planet. We have collectively had problems in distribution, blocked by political and ideological fixed ideas. Any lack of supply is simply a lack of creative solution.

"Enemies" to organizations do not factually exist. Where any organization uses such attitudes toward others, it factually is working to destroy that same organization. Competition injures both competitors and their shared public. Monopolistic ideas also simply hurt that very public the company is supposed to be servicing and selling to. Where companies are trying to "make money" or "stockpile assets," it is way off the mark.

Those who gain greater market share, greater public to consume its product, simply provide greater, more complete solution than others. Often, this means inclusion of other firms as by merger. However, much time can be wasted in simply trying to defend or attack these solutions and their companies or individuals. Practically, the only real defense is to come up with a better solution. However, competition – maligned into the sole definition of survival of the fittest – has been misinterpreted. Mixing hatred or antagonism into the fray simply slows greater solution to any given problem, any given situation. So models which base economics on war or violent behavior of any type (such as animal behavior in the wild) are simply delusions spread by destructive individuals.

There are two simple datums which describe economics:

Go Thunk Yourself!

1. The purpose of any company is to deliver a service to individuals, directly or indirectly, in a remunerative fashion so that it can continue to deliver a service.

2. These individuals work out and produce an exchange for these services so as to improve their quality of life.

From violations and alterations of these two statements, one can derive all the faults of modern economic and political thought. As well, one can streamline existing businesses to improve their delivery. Politics could learn these datums, since Western governments often violate the rights of the individual to produce that exchange – anything given away for free isn't valuable to the individual; as well, taxes on companies in excess of what is needed to preserve public, common goods' value only limit the businesses ability to deliver their chosen service. After all, businesses are just organized groups of individuals (who each work their for their exchange to improve their quality of life, etc.) Excessive taxes create overhead costs which cause the company to take action to reduce these costs to ensure their survival. Often these solutions in our modern, footloose societies mean moving to another state or another country. This harms the survival of the individuals who directly participate in that company to aid their own survival. Most of these solutions depend on passing on these increased costs to their buyers and/or their workers. The balance is the maintenance of the public goods against the survival of the company. In our present Information Age, solutions are being found with more and more rapidity, requiring similar evolving rapidity within the individuals connected to these companies. And so these test our basic social bedrock and require these to evolve more rapidly than ever before.

Governments and businesses could be more creative and more responsible in resolving their solutions. But they as well must work to be less competitive and more pro-active.

Taxing the rich to pay the poor only ensures the poor stay that way. The rich aren't made any less rich through taxes alone. Taxing the rich to provide effective training that the poor can afford in order to learn how to become rich might be a better solution. But handouts don't work and never have. Equitable loans honestly repaid have. Teaching people to fish has kept people fed over the eons.

The idea of the Golden Rule is then a workable economic one. It is not, perhaps, the best solution possible, but it works historically and has wide support. Anyone can prove that it works for themselves. A model of executing this might be found in the Open Source movement, which is consistently gaining ground on the status quo. Imagine, a group of people who almost completely work for free and who constantly have the challenge of simply improving the quality of their application – and these better solutions gain greater public use (market share). But those who champion other solutions limit their own survival to the degree they incorporate these into their mission statement/vision.

So, basing business and personal solutions on this one datum is a safe (and profitable) one. Governmental employees, particularly appointed and elected ones, should take this to heart, as well as labor unions. All should work to see others around them as associates and partners in building creative cooperation to solve the various difficulties they encounter. This would build a true Golden Age.

This book hopefully lays the groundwork to make this possible.

I include these brief notes as additional thoughts on this subject. Certainly this book is no last work, nothing more than an introduction to a very wide subject. More books are needed on this subject. But I hope to have contributed to opening some doors of thought for others that we all might lead more successful lives.

Robert C. Worstell

Dr. Robert C. Worstell

Part II – The Original Study

I include here a description of the study done in order to distill these 14 points. I submitted this as part of the requirements for a Master's Degree. I did the study, wrote the book as part of testing that data and then after some years of additional research, used that study to base this thesis. I include it for those who like to dig deeper and who would like to see more of the original research.

Dr. Robert C. Worstell

The Search for an Underlying Core System Behind Self-Help Bestsellers

by Robert C. Worstell

(Master's Thesis
Approved July 16, 2006)

Introduction

"God helps them who help themselves."
Benjamin Franklin – The Way to Wealth

"Self-help" is a modern phrase venue where people in our modern age can popularly immerse themselves in successful metaphysical formulas and disciplines without having to confront the stigma of Established Religion or Academia, both of which have thoroughly inoculated their participants narrowly into their own "vertical silos" of dogmatic thought. These modern books are phrased in popular vernacular to appeal to an audience which has been steeped in Western Objective Science, not necessarily Eastern Mysticism.

I undertook a study of popular and effective self-help books to determine if there were a single common system of self-help which ran throughout bestselling self-improvement books. While any of us undoubtedly have our own system of beliefs which serves us in this area, I sought to determine if any common system were popularly supported, at least in our Western culture. Such understanding would be of valuable use, since any such underlying system would show both the efficacy of such a system and also how our culture is currently treating and is being introduced to the self-help field.

All of the candidate books were successful long after their first edition and most are being reprinted and sold even today, some of them hundreds of years after their authors died. That was the criterion: they had to be still in circulation or best sellers long after their authors died – showing that people generally still found them useful and workable, not dependent on the personal magnetism of the author.

In this paper, I distill each of these books to their various key basics. I then see if there were enough common principles in use that an obvious system underlay them. These system basics are reviewed to see if they do compose an underlying system. Then the background sources of the authors are investigated to see if these were stemming from a common philosophical school. A tertiary cross-check is then done with current best-selling self-help books (whose author is living) to see if the commonalities held. The possible applications of this system and its points are then investigated.

Review of Literature

I. The Basis of This Study

This study was initially made up of best selling self-help classics who continued to sell and be distributed widely (for free in many cases) after the author's death. This gave us three key criteria:

1. The text was found appealing to its audience and purchased widely.

2. The text is continuing to be found as useful, regardless of grammar, language or style changes.

3. The sales of the book didn't depend on the personal charisma of the author or social fads and whims.

These requisites produced a list of books which gave a body of data consistently found useful and workable by their readers. Their immense and continuing popular support showed that they had each a very workable and prized philosophy. That was the premise of the study: there were possibly common datums in use throughout self-help texts that could lead to a single common philosophy or even a science of self-improvement – something that anyone could and would apply and use, since these were probably based on naturally occurring laws.

This list was derived from searches for self-help and finding through Amazon and other large booksellers what is currently best selling, looking for works continuing to be republished after their authors' death. Searches were also done for historical bestsellers (not necessarily currently on bestseller lists, but having set sales/distribution records) as a cross-check. All books on this list at one time were bestsellers, which sales records extended well beyond their author's death.

The works which did make the short list were widely applicable, encompassing not only wealth, but success in life in general. Several addressed personal health, prosperity, and other quality of life issues which have been common to mankind through the eons, not just a single generation. But they are simple to understand and use simple, down-to-earth examples. So there is the commonality of universal application in addition to a simply read and understood work.

I ignored current bestselling fads in self-improvement, such as the entire genre of diet books and any fictional works.

The books which made this list:

Allen, James. As A Man Thinketh. DeVorss & Co. Oct 1983.

Carnegie, Dale. How to Win Friends and Influence People. Pocket Books. May 1990.

Clason, George S. The Richest Man in Babylon. Penguin Books, Signet. Feb 1988

Ghazzali, Al. <u>The Alchemy of Happiness</u>
Cosimo Classics, Nov 2005

Haanel, Charles F. <u>Master Key System</u>.
Kallisti Publishing. Jan 2000.

Hill, Napoleon. <u>Think and Grow Rich.</u>
Fawcett Books. November 1990.

Peale, Norman Vincent. <u>The Power of Positive Thinking</u>. Ballentine, Fawcett, Del Ray, Ivy. June 1982

Wattles, Wallace D. <u>The Science of Getting Rich</u>. Iceni Books. Jan 2002.

Studying these books showed recurring points, which were noted. While there were over a dozen key points, not all points showed up in all books. Any system would have a majority of the points; a few of these books did. On completing all these studies, I then looked up current bestsellers to see if I had any comparative work s which were similar in sales magnitude. Only one had a sales record outstanding enough to compare to these historical bestsellers and so qualify as a cross-reference:

Covey, Stephen. <u>The 7 Habits of Highly Effective People</u>. Free Press, Simon and Schuster. 1989.

His text was found to have the same data as the older texts and so contributed proof to the study's premise.

Here is the list of 14 points derived from the studied works. They were given a single word descriptive and short definition, to aid in study.

The points:

1. REASON: A reason to change, something to shoot for, goal.
2. THINK: One has the capability of independent thought.
3. CHANGE: A person can change his own attitudes.
4. MIND: The surrounding environment is resultant from the mental environment.
5. POSITIVE: Emphasis on positive outlook on life – eliminating critical thought and behavior.
6. ACHIEVE: One can accomplish personal control over being, doing, achieving and acquiring.
7. GOLDEN RULE: Underlying moral/ethical understanding – operating in a non-competitive manner.
8. VISION: Being able to envision personal goals and outcomes to achieve.
9. ACTION: Developing and putting plans into effect to achieve one's vision.

Go Thunk Yourself!

10. FAITH: An internally created energy which supports a personal belief system.

11. AFFIRMATION: Use of affirmations to strengthen faith.

12. POWER THROUGH PRAYER: Belief in a Supreme Being or Higher Power; Prayer/meditation as a method of increasing one's personal effectiveness.

13. PEACE: Peace of Mind through self-control.

14. MASTER MIND: Surround yourself with people around you who think as you do. Composite mind will achieve the composite vision shared.

I created a chart to study these points. I was then able to pick the most representative works for more in-depth study and also verify the frequency of how these points showed up across these works.

The texts (in no certain order) are assigned letters:

    A: Letter to Garcia, by Elbert Hubbard

    B: The Way to Wealth, by Benjamin Franklin

    C: Science of Getting Rich, by Wallace D. Wattles

    D: How to Win Friends and Influence People, by Dale Carnegie

    E: As a Man Thinketh, by James Allen

    F: Master Key System, by Charles F. Haanel

G: Think and Grow Rich, by Napoleon Hill

H: The Alchemy of Happiness, by Al Ghazzali

I: The Richest Man in Babylon, by George S. Clason

J: The 7 Habits of Highly Effective People, by Stephan R. Covey

K: The Power of Positive Thinking, by Norman Vincent Peale

	1	2	3	4	5	6	7	8	9	10	11	12	13	14	%
A													x		7
B	x			x			x								21
C	x	x	x	x	x	x	x	x	x	x	x	x	x	x	100
D		x		x	x										21
E	x	x	x	x	x	x	x	x	x			x	x		78
F	x	x	x	x	x	x	x	x	x	x	x	x	x	x	100
G	x	x	x	x	x	x	x	x	x		x	x	x	x	92
H							x					x			14
I	x							x	x					x	29
J	x	x	x	x	x	x	x	x	x	x	x	x	x	x	100
K	x	x	x	x		x	x			x			x	x	64
%	72.7	54.5	54.5	72.2	45.5	63.3	72.2	63.3	54.5	36.3	36.3	63.3	54.5	54.5	

One can see that three of these stand out: C: Science of Getting Rich, F: Master Key System, and J: 7 Habits of Highly Effective People. After this come G: Think and Grow Rich, E: As a Man Thinketh, K: Power of Positive Thinking, H: The Alchemy of Happiness, B: The Way to Wealth and D: How to Win Friends and Influence People, then finally A: Letter to Garcia.

Go Thunk Yourself!

The key recurring points 1 (Reason), 4 (Mind), and 7 (Golden Rule). Three others follow, 6 (Achieve), 8 (Vision), and 12 (Prayer). Five others are over fifty percent, 2 (Think), 3 (Change), 9 (Action), 13 (Peace), 14 (Master Mind). In the minority are 5 (Positive), 10 (Faith), 11 (Affirmation). That some books held more in common doesn't reflect particularly on the importance of any given point. Those three books who do touch all points have a power in their works not approached in the others.

The key summary point is that three books, written at different times by different authors who did not know each other came up with the same key principles (however, Covey mentioned in his book that he studied some 200 years of self-help literature in preparation for writing his book and so would probably have studied most all of these). That six points are common to over two-thirds of these books points to some underlying system of self-help exists through popular literature.

Such individual standings do not tell the relative effectiveness of the books. Most of these are about making wealth, which is a much-marketed factor in Western Civilization in the supposed creating of happiness. Others, such as Ghazzali's work, and Peale's are more along a religious bent. Where one wants to get data on how to become wealthy or how to improve one's character, or get more faith into one's life, the above books have individual approaches to these specific points.

Several of these are distinguished by sales in their own right. Franklin was probably the first best-selling self-help author on this continent, over 200,000 copies when printing itself was in its infancy in the American colonies. Ghazzali showed up during a search for historically popular self-help works; his work is perhaps the first work known as in this genre historically. Hubbard's short work sold over 40 million copies as many, many copies were purchased and given away by plant owners to their employees.

Certainly, there is some personal decision factor in my analysis of these books. But I've taken the key points and tried not to run in some interpretation (such as faith and planning would be required to achieve the teamwork result in <u>Letter to Garcia</u> – in this book, the emphasis was entirely on popularizing the action of being a team member).

These books simply have a common message through them. I've been able to take historical and current day bestselling self-help texts and derive key points which show an apparent underlying set of commonly used elements for a possible self-help system.

II. Brief History and Apparent Origin of American Self-Help Classics

While these books differ in location written and time period, they do have a similar philosophic influence.

These books cover over 70 years between the earliest and latest. The latest, Covey's <u>7 Habits</u> (1989), was based on his study of 200 years of self-help texts in America. In the 20th century we have Peale's <u>Positive Thinking</u> (1952), preceded by Hill's <u>Think and Grow Rich</u> (1937) and Dale Carnegie's <u>How to Win Friends</u> (1937). Twenty years earlier is James Allen's <u>As A Man Thinketh</u> (1902), Charles F. Haanel's <u>Master Key System</u> (1912) and Wallace D. Wattles' <u>Science of Getting Rich</u> (1910).

Possible influences on these works can't be attributed directly to the environmental influences of their times. Peale's influence might have been the Cold War mentality of the late 40's and early 50's. Hill, while starting his research twenty years earlier, published during the depression for the stated purpose of getting enabling people to start making money again. As well, this was the publishing time of Dale Carnegie. Allen published after World War I, while Haanel and Wattles published prior, during America's affluence period. While the latter works all might be touted as responses to war and recovery, this theory doesn't hold for the earliest works, whose authors had never seen a whole world at war.

A more interesting line of approach to determine commonalities is the principles which have surfaced in the different books. Most of these authors are known to be included as classics under the umbrella of "New Thought." According to a pamphlet originally distributed by the Calgary New Thought Center, Peale is also included as being heavily influenced by New Thought authors. Haanel himself references Judge (Thomas) Troward who lectured and wrote widely on the subject of "Mental Science" from 1902 to his death in 1916. The Calgary pamphlet credits Troward with being one of the two "taproots" of the New Thought movement. Calgary's other taproot was Phineas P. Quimby, who cured and trained many healers, who in turn were able to train others, forming organizations and churches as they spread, forming the current churches of New Thought lineage.

Franklin, Ghazzali and Clason are not connected with New Thought by any record. Hubbard may have had some connection with Emerson or Alcott, who were on the history-line of New Thought, via the Transcendentalists.

New Thought is itself inclusive of a wide-ranging span of thoughts and ideas, ranging from mystic to biblical to scientific and everything in between. It currently has perhaps the greatest collection of modern thinkers and philosophers under its broad umbrella, these working as well to modernize concepts found in ancient Eastern texts for a modern Western audience. It's not surprising particularly that New Thought ideas would then influence self-help so widely. What is surprising is that this one philosophic school would sprout continuing best sellers and/or be the source for underlying principles of self-improvement. Since New Thought is inclusive of modern analysis and ancient works beyond Greek and also history's oldest written works, this says much about its openness and the workability of the included theories and practices. Narrowly dogmatic philosophic schools which tend to exclude would not be broadly applicable outside its narrow belief-system and followers.

We now have a set of recurring self-help principles which are popularly supported and an underlying philosophic school on which these elements are based. The next point of inquiry is how these are possibly a system. That one philosophic school is capable of being a base for all the historical self-help bestsellers predisposes us to believe that these elements are part of an underlying system of self-help.

The trick to this is that New Thought, not being a centrally-organized operation, isn't popularly publicized or advertised as a key philosophic source in modern society. Certain New Thought churches are able to publicize themselves locally, but nothing on a scale which would support or effect nationwide book sales of even a single book over several decades. What is interesting is where certain popular books are able to distill the body of New Thought beliefs down to a simple set of elements which are readily communicated and assimilated by the reading public. It is also interesting that these are repetitively executed by different authors in different ages, under different socio-economic conditions. This predicts that a possible underlying popular system has been selected by the reading public. The elements I've described above might be part or all of such a popular system.

Next, I'll examine how these elements may work with each other to develop such a system.

Findings

Mentioned earlier, I was in search of a possible underlying system. That I found a small handful of common points didn't mean anything unless they were proved useful. Taking into mind the views of these authors, I worked to arrange these items in a logical fashion, so that simpler and basic ideas would then set the foundation for later ideas. That these individual pieces then hold together coherently tends to show the existence of an underlying system.

These points in order:

1. REASON: A reason to change, something to shoot for, goal.

Before anything can change, there needs to be a reason for change. Nothing in this universe is unmotivated, if only by the need for entertainment or distraction from boredom. The reader would have to decide to take responsibility for his/her own situation and decide to to something about it.

2. THINK: You can think for yourself.

Next would be requiring/inviting the person to start thinking for him/herself, to decide on the basis of personal experience what they wanted to do with their life. While most modern readers have been deluged with mind-numbing advertisements from their first TV show, it is essential that any reader be able to know that they could think on their own in order to decide to change their mind.

3. CHANGE: A person can change his own attitudes

This point, which goes back at least to Aristotle and popularized by Carnegie and others, is a key point. A person has a reason for change, knows he/she can change his own thoughts and now finds that his/her emotions and attitudes can be altered at will, simply by practicing facial expressions to do so. Here, the reader is being made again more self-sufficient and independent of the world around him/her.

The mental state of a person will affect the decisions he/she makes in life. Feelings of hopelessness will result in apathetic decisions to do nothing about it and be a victim. Fear will prompt a person to simply retreat from doing anything, or take the easiest, less painful way out. Anger might make a person decide to attack or criticize, saying things one might regret later on. The interested, even enthusiastic person will decide in terms of the best solution that benefits the majority concerned and perhaps even work out how to make a profit from that situation.

Here also, the reader is introduced to not hanging on to negative emotions which have nagged that person their entire life. There are many exercises in these books which enable a person to get over such emotional problems simply by changing their minds by decision.

4. MIND: The surrounding environment is a result of the mental environment.

Now the reader can be introduced to a key concept because of the logic of the preceding three points. Allen and others had this as basically the key and only point which their book was based on: the physical environment around a person can be changed by changing that person's mental environment.

While this point is familiar to any reader of self-help or metaphysical texts, here we see that this can be logically introduced once one knows that his own thoughts can be brought under his control. This can be illustrated by showing how his/her mental attitudes created emotional scenes in his/her life, which could have been avoided entirely. Allen and Haanel have more specific examples of the technical reasons this is a rock-solid datum, verifiable through the most objective scientific experiments.

For our use, it is key only that the reader is able inductively to agree with the concept and start using it in his/her life.

5. ACHIEVE: Personal control is possible over being, doing, achieving and acquiring.

Since thought is under control and creates the external universe, if only through the action of creating one's own attitudes, then personal achievement is basically limitless, providing no physical handicap is present. Again, a logical step.

6. POSITIVE: Emphasis on positive outlook on life — eliminating critical thought and behavior.

While this seems a needless comment, it actually isn't. Most of the modern society is filled with criticisms and needling. Advertising is built on people having low self-esteem and self-confidence and staying that way. Were people to make up their own mind and decide to act positively at all times in all manners, they would need far fewer pills and weight-loss guides.

This is another logical step, since people who can think and decide for themselves, who have something they want to achieve – these can now step up to the plate and decide to act only or mostly positively in improving their lives.

7. GOLDEN RULE: Underlying moral/ethical understanding is the base for self-help

As we've found that positive, creative thought is more vital, more effective than non-positive, non-creative thought – this leads logically to the next step: in order to make the best decisions, the most profitable ones, we have to treat others like we would like to be treated.

Again, while the vast majority of religions have this datum enshrined in their scriptures, it isn't a common operating basis in this planet. It again is built on the prior points, but is required to be decidedly stated so that people can have an ethical base to choose how to create their attitudes and where to take their lives.

8. VISION: Visions are composed of hopes and dreams; they create reality.

Here the reader is now introduced to the stuff which apparently drives this universe. The personal vision which people hold in front of them is what they mirror their universe to be. Having a complete vision supplements your chosen goal and is actually a broader statement of it. Seeing this goal in all its details makes it much easier to achieve and make manifest in the world around one.

Again, we are continuing to increase the ability of the reader by giving him more bite-sized chunks which logically ensue from the earlier steps.

9. ACTION: Putting plans into effect will achieve one's vision.

Why daydreams are so disregarded is the simple fact that they are usually never planned out for actualization, no action is taken on them. If a long journey is planned out, but that first step is never taken, it is only a nicely laid out plan.

This follows vision as a vital explanation as to why affirmations often get a bad name: you can't simply mouth the words for improvement and then do nothing to actually achieve what you really want. So the reader is now told he has to get off his chair and do something with his life.

10. FAITH: Faith is self-generated, self-created.

Faith is self-generated. Part of creating a new environment around the reader depends on how much self-confidence or self-trust can be created. If the person distrusts his own plan or his abilities to carry it out, then no positive change will be accomplished. The reader at this point is reminded again that this is SELF-help and so one has to have faith in one-SELF to get the vision executed for real.

11. AFFIRMATION: Affirmations can be used to strengthen faith and achieve your vision.

Only now can the reader effectively start to use affirmations. The need for change is evident, the reader knows he/she can do it if change is really wanted. There is a vision and plan in place to achieve it. The reader now can generate his own self-confidence and self-trust. By now writing out and/or speaking key points to that vision, it is easier to manifest that vision in the here and now.

12. POWER THROUGH PRAYER: Belief in a Supreme Being or Higher Power – tapping into one's relationship with the Supreme Being increases one's own abilities and power.

This point is an empirical one. All my studies here and later have consistently run into this exact point in self-help studies. None failed to mention this as a key element, while they might have different names (Higher Intelligence, Universal Mind, et al.). Dr. Peale gives many useful exercises down this line, although all the books tie the effectiveness of self-help to this, directly or indirectly.

Setting this point here simply builds on the ideas of vision and faith above. Introducing it as a prior point would only possibly alienate some readers who have had dogmatic experiences with particular religions. Most people agree there is some sort of Supreme Being or Higher Intelligence at work. Mentioning this at this point should only get agreement minimally, but can increase the effects of the planning and actions in manifesting the vision of the individual markedly.

13. PEACE: Peace of Mind is attainable through self-control.

This follows logically from understanding the connection of self-improvement with a Supreme Being, but isn't necessarily dependent on such. Later studies give a far greater detailed understanding of why this works this way. For our purposes, we would show the reader what he/she should be expecting and how to fine tune his/her vision, planning and action to get the maximal personal gain out of these. Additionally, working from a stably peaceful mind will be far more efficient in manifesting his/her goal.

14. MASTER MIND: Surround yourself with people around you who think as you do. The composite mind will achieve the composite vision shared.

Now the reader can include others in on the plan to make it happen on a broader scale than that single individual could achieve by himself. But until one is rock-solid with the vision, planning and underlying self-confident attitude, only then should one start to bring others on board.

This then presents a system of self-help on a logical gradient. I'm sure that a simple system could be built with fewer elements. But on review, one can see that while several could be included under a single heading, having specific emphasis on every point here makes the entire system more workable and easier to train through gradient study. (Haanel, of note, had 24 gradient lessons in his <u>Master Key System</u> course of study.)

While no system is infallible, that one could cross-compare various other bestselling authors and find the bulk or all the above elements present points to a probable underlying system used by these authors. Similarly, where you examine the cheap rip-off editions of self-help, they lack a real understanding of the basics outlined above. Certainly one could bridge from these workable basics into more specialized and extensive training into meditation, for example, or the specifics of financing as gone over by Clason.

Discussion

There are certain observations and remarks that can be, and should be made regarding self-help and the system discovered as a whole, as well as potential applications of it to broader areas such as society and government.

1. This study brings about an understanding of how to reach the reading public. Many have been inured to anything but the purest objective science. They have similarly been warned about studying anything but their own church's belief system. Academic writings generally are too erudite and professorial in approach to be readily understood or appreciated by a general public.

So the language has to be neutral, simple and effective. The most consistent bestsellers manage to keep the sentences direct and simple and so have managed to make the 100-year shift in culture and language.

The point of religion has been approached my several of these authors in a circumspect manner. Exceptions are Covey and particularly Peale. But Peale doesn't forward a particular dogma, while he obviously is approaching from a Protestant viewpoint, his very practical exercises and examples enable anyone to achieve their self-help goals through prayer and religious experience – all without Bible-thumping or dogmatic preaching.

In short, the language of these successful authors is very much man on the street and clear. Most people believe in God and pray as part of that belief. So mentioning God, a Supreme Being or Divine Will isn't a death knell to book sales. The point is to write in a very real manner and make logical sense, plus forward simple and useful practices which can be readily applied.

2. Logic says that practically there are no limits to what one can achieve with this system. For as one continues to work, that person will find that there are fewer and fewer limits as he goes, perhaps finding that more of these are grounded in the physical plane than spiritual. As human thought, as assisted by the Universal Mind, is practically limitless, so the potential human ability level which can be achieved is likewise unlimited. While more can be said about this, it is well understood by any regular practitioner in the subject and is better used in forming the support for the next argument.

Making these books widely available could increase the amount of highly able people on this planet, bringing more artists and skilled counselor-types to view and to work on the problems this society faces every minute of our 24-hour days.

3. The nature of the system described in these books demands one evolve a synergy between the subconscious (per Haanel and others), the conscious spirit/soul which inhabits the body and the Divine. Covey devotes an entire chapter to this concept. "Creative

cooperation" he also calls it. Other studies either tend to confuse the body and the spirit or try to ignore the Divine influence by being "scientific" about it. Practically, more and more scientific studies are beginning to recognize the limits of pure materialistic research, i.e., denying any causation that cannot occur outside of strictly physical limits. But as well, the role of intuition has been determined to be integral to science's breakthroughs. Intuition requires all three factors of the subconscious, conscious and Divine minds to operate in cooperation. Studies in Huna (the Polynesian religio-social philosophic system which predates Eastern sources to New Thought) confirm the interrelationship of these three points.

Another factor in such a synergy would be purpose. For what reason is the action occurring? What are you trying to accomplish? We deal still with the objective part of this – that of the conscious mind – to determine this purpose, in alignment with the Divine and the limits to the facilities of the subconscious. One can have all sorts of different purposes, either constructive or non-constructive (destructive), positive or non-positive (negative). I describe these in these terms to show the practical applications. Construct means literally to build together and destruct means to build apart. Both are based on the point of create, one creating cooperatively and the other creating divisively. The optimal purpose and resultant solution would generate tremendous support and solve various problems both in the present and in the future.

4. The final point I am leading up to is that readers of these books have this advantage: they can use this data to create immensely

useful corporate, governmental and religious organizations, quite in addition to personal gain. Were just the five books containing the bulk of the elements gotten into continuous consumption by people on this planet, not just this Western culture, many admirable and positive effects could be created. Where the original authors are referenced, a greater veracity could be achieved for such a self-help system, as it isn't a single author who is the source of this data, but a systemic body of work which cross-references itself.

Once a body of practicing public were achieved, many international problems would disappear or be greatly alleviated. War, starvation and many political/governmental ills could be reduce if not erased as people were able to implement the above system or some version of it. Popular opinion would force governmental revision toward more accountability and effective action based on moral, not political gain. Independent financial donations would ease natural disasters through popularly-supported relief. Several of these books mention the idea of what would happen if the majority of the populace started treating each other with mutual respect and honesty. We would have a very peaceful cultural revolution, all without firing a shot or any required government action.

Governments and businesses could be more creative and more responsible in resolving their solutions. But they as well must work to be less competitive and more pro-active. The shareholders in both need to exercise their own understanding of how to achieve more through cooperation than competition. Getting such bestsellers in use by leaders of these groups would make the businesses more profitable and the governments more honest and accountable. Governmental employees, particularly appointed and elected ones, should take this to heart, as well as corporate executives. All should work to see others around them as associates and partners in building creative cooperation to solve the various difficulties they encounter. This could build a true Golden Age.

Working within a self-help system as outlined above has far more reaching effects than just personal gain. So I included these brief sociological observations as additional thoughts on this subject.

Summary and Conclusions

In this paper, I've examined the bestselling self-help authors of this century and derived both a popular system of self-improvement elements. I've traced these authors influences to New Thought philosophies. The elements themselves were shown to be logically inductive to the formation of a personal effective belief-system. Along with the popular vernacular used by these authors, their inherent effective value gives ample reason for their record sales.

There are perhaps no factual limits to what can be accomplished in using these principles, this system, these books. Logically, one could see that there are no real barriers to an individual's thoughts and imagination, so conceivably no limit to what could be accomplished in the physical universe.

Even while Haanel above points out that one cannot change another for him, while Wattles warns not to get into occult practices in an effort to change another against their will, Peale also tells us a story where a woman restored her marriage and avoided divorce through the above principles, Covey tells of deciding to handle a disruptive conflict he was having for months with an associate – only to find that the associate wanted to handle it as well. One doesn't know what another wants particularly, through using the tools above – visualization, faith, prayer, action – many, many inter-social and inter-cultural affairs can be resolved. One doesn't know that the other doesn't want to change or improve – your work would minimally give them that chance.

Several of the authors (Haanel, Peale, Wattles) say to think and visualize as big as you can, that these make the smaller problems fall away as insignificant. With the application of the principle involved in the "Master Mind," a wide association of individuals with the common ideal will achieve many, widespread – even global effects. One such example is the view of Human Rights, which started with Locke, Jefferson and the Founding Fathers, then was spread through the globe due to the efforts of the United States UN delegate, Eleanor Roosevelt, who drafted and got agreement from other delegates enough to sign it into a UN resolution – all from her New York apartment. Now this is a held standard across the globe. One by one, countries are being persuaded to accede to this thought, this vision which is shared now by so many internationally. Global human rights would be achieved far more quickly were the principles in the above books commonly understood and applied across this planet.

Certainly this paper is no final approach to the subject self-help or the books referenced; this paper is nothing more than an introductory look at a very wide subject. Each of these books can be studied time and time again to gain more application and results. More papers and books are ever welcome on this subject. We already have a start with the above best-selling self-help books which have already been written. It can be seen that dissemination of any such basic self-help is vital to this age for survival of both our personal selves and our international organizations.

Robert C. Worstell - Jan. 14, 2006

Bibliography

Allen, James. As A Man Thinketh.
        DeVorss & Co. Oct 1983.

Carnegie, Dale. How to Win Friends and Influence People.
        Pocket Books. May 1990.

Clason, George S. The Richest Man in Babylon.
        Penguin Books, Signet. Feb 1988

Covey, Stephen. The 7 Habits of Highly Effective People.
        Free Press, Simon and Schuster. 1989.

Hill, Napoleon. Think and Grow Rich.
        Fawcett Books. November 1990.

Haanel, Charles F. Master Key System.
        Kallisti Publishing. Jan 2000.

Peale, Norman Vincent. The Power of Positive Thinking.
        Ballentine, Fawcett, Del Ray, Ivy. June 1982

Troward, Thomas. <u>The Edinburgh and Dore Lectures on Mental Science</u>.
Arthur Vergara. 1989.

Wattles, Wallace D. <u>The Science of Getting Rich</u>.
Iceni Books. Jan 2002.

Ghazzali, Al. <u>The Alchemy of Happiness</u>
Kitabwala. January 2000.

Part III – Bonus Section

As a Man Thinketh,
by James Allen

and

A Summary of The Science of Getting Rich,
by Wallace D. Wattles

and

Master Key System Study Questions with Answers
by Charles F. Haanel

Dr. Robert C. Worstell

As A Man Thinketh

by

James Allen

(originally published in 1902)

Mind is the Master power that moulds and makes,
And Man is Mind, and evermore he takes
The tool of Thought, and, shaping what he wills,
Brings forth a thousand joys, a thousand ills:--
He thinks in secret, and it comes to pass:
Environment is but his looking-glass.

Forward

This little volume (the result of meditation and experience) is not intended as an exhaustive treatise on the much-written-upon subject of the power of thought. It is suggestive rather than explanatory, its object being to stimulate men and women to the discovery and perception of the truth that —

"They themselves are makers of themselves"

by virtue of the thoughts which they choose and encourage; that mind is the master weaver, both of the inner garment of character and the outer garment of circumstance, and that, as they may have hitherto woven in ignorance and pain they may now weave in enlightenment and happiness.

James Allen

Ilfracombe, England

Chapter One

As A Man Thinketh

The aphorism, "As a man thinketh in his heart so is he," not only embraces the whole of a man's being, but is so comprehensive as to reach out to every condition and circumstance of his life. A man is literally **what he thinks**, his character being the complete sum of all his thoughts.

As the plant springs from, and could not be without, the seed, so every act of a man springs from the hidden seeds of thought, and could not have appeared without them. This applies equally to those acts called "spontaneous" and "unpremeditated" as to those which are deliberately executed.

Act is the blossom of thought, and joy and suffering are its fruits; thus does a man garner in the sweet and bitter produce of his own husbandry.

> "Thought in the mind hath made us, What we are
> By thought was wrought and built. If a man's mind
> Hath evil thoughts, pain comes on him as comes
> The wheel the ox behind....

> ..If one endure
> In purity of thought, joy follows him
> As his own shadow--sure."

Man is a growth by law, and not a creation by artifice, and cause and effect is as absolute and undeviating in the hidden realm of thought as in the world of visible and material things. A noble and Godlike character is not a thing of favor or chance, but is the natural result of continued effort in right thinking, the effect of long-cherished association with Godlike thoughts. An ignoble and bestial character, by the same process, is the result of the continued harboring of groveling thoughts.

Man is made or unmade by himself; in the armory of thought he forges the weapons by which he destroys himself. He also fashions the tools with which he builds for himself heavenly mansions of joy and strength and peace. By the right choice and true application of thought, man ascends to the Divine Perfection; by the abuse and wrong application of thought, he descends below the level of the beast. Between these two extremes are all the grades of character, and man is their maker and master.

Of all the beautiful truths pertaining to the soul which have been restored and brought to light in this age, none is more gladdening or fruitful of divine promise and confidence than this - that man is the master of thought, the molder of character, and maker and shaper of condition, environment, and destiny.

As a being of Power, Intelligence, and Love, and the lord of his own thoughts, man holds the key to every situation, and contains within himself that transforming and regenerative agency by which he may make himself what he wills.

Man is always the master, even in his weakest and most abandoned state; but in his weakness and degradation he is the foolish master who misgoverns his "household." When he begins to reflect upon his condition, and to search diligently for the Law upon which his being is established, he then becomes the wise master, directing his energies with intelligence, and fashioning his thoughts to fruitful issues. Such is the **conscious** master, and man can only thus become by discovering **within himself** the laws of thought; which discovery is totally a matter of application, self-analysis, and experience.

Only by much searching and mining are gold an diamonds obtained, and man can find every truth connected with his being if he will dig deep into the mine of his soul. And that he is the maker of his character, the molder of his life, and the builder of his destiny, he may unerringly prove: if he will watch, control, and alter his thoughts, tracing their effects upon himself, upon others, and upon his life and circumstances; if he will link cause and effect by patient practice and investigation, utilizing his every experience, even to the most trivial, as a means of obtaining that knowledge of himself. In this direction, as in no other, is the law absolute that "He that seeketh findeth; and to him that knocketh it shall be opened"; for only by patience, practice, and ceaseless importunity can a man enter the Door of the Temple of Knowledge.

Dr. Robert C. Worstell

Chapter Two

Effect of Thought on Circumstances

A man's mind may be likened to a garden, which may be intelligently cultivated or allowed to run wild; but whether cultivated or neglected, it must, and will, **bring forth**. If no useful seeds are **put** into it, then an abundance of useless weed seeds will **fall** therein, and will continue to produce their kind.

Just as a gardener cultivates his plot, keeping it free from weeds, and growing the flowers and fruits which he requires, so may a man tend the garden of his mind, weeding out all the wrong, useless, and impure thoughts, and cultivating toward perfection the flowers and fruits of right, useful, and pure thoughts, By pursuing this process, a man sooner or later discovers that he is the master gardener of his soul, the director of his life. He also reveals, within himself, the laws of thought, and understands with ever-increasing accuracy, how the thought forces and mind elements operate in the shaping of his character, circumstances, and destiny.

Thought and character are one, and as character can only manifest and discover itself through environment and circumstance, the outer conditions of a person's life will always be found to be harmoniously related to his inner state. This does not mean that a man's circumstances at any given time are an indication of his **entire** character, but that those circumstances are so intimately connected with some vital thought element within himself that, for the time being, they are indispensable to his development.

Every man is where he is by the law of his being. The thoughts which he has built into his character have brought him there, and in the arrangement of his life there is no element of chance, but all is the result of a law which cannot err. This is just as true of those who feel "out of harmony" with their surroundings as of those who are contented with them.

As the progressive and evolving being, man is where he is that he may learn that he may grow; and as he learns the spiritual lesson which any circumstance contains for him, it passes away and gives place to other circumstances.

Man is buffeted by circumstances so long as he believes himself to be the creature of outside conditions. But when he realizes that he may command the hidden soil and seeds of his being out of which circumstances grow, he then becomes the rightful master of himself.

That circumstances grow out of thought every man knows who has for any length of time practiced self-control and self-purification, for he will have noticed that the alteration in his circumstances has been in exact ratio with his altered mental condition. So true is this that when a man earnestly applies himself to remedy the defects in his character, and makes swift and marked progress, he passes rapidly through a succession of vicissitudes.

The soul attracts that which it secretly harbors; that which it loves, and also that which it fears. It reaches the height of its cherished aspirations. It falls to the level of its unchastened desires - and circumstances are the means by which the soul receives its own.

Every thought seed sown or allowed to fall into the mind, and to take root there, produces its own, blossoming sooner or later into act, and bearing its own fruitage of opportunity and circumstance. Good thoughts bear good fruit, bad thoughts bad fruit.

The outer world of circumstance shapes itself to the inner world of thought, and both pleasant and unpleasant external conditions are factors which make for the ultimate good of the individual. As the reaper of his own harvest, man learns both by suffering and bliss.

A man does not come to the almshouse or the jail by the tyranny of fate of circumstance, but by the pathway of groveling thoughts and base desires. Nor does a pure-minded man fall suddenly into crime by stress of any mere external force; the criminal thought had long been secretly fostered in the heart, and the hour of opportunity revealed its gathered power.

Circumstance does not make the man; it reveals him to himself. No such conditions can exist as descending into vice and its attendant sufferings apart from vicious inclinations, or ascending into virtue and its pure happiness without the continued cultivation of virtuous aspirations. And man, therefore, as the Lord and master of thought, is the maker of himself, the shaper and author of environment. Even at birth the soul comes to its own, and through every step of its earthly pilgrimage it attracts those combinations of conditions which reveal itself, which are the reflections of its own purity and impurity, its strength and weakness.

Men do not attract that which they **want**, but that which they **are**. Their whims, fancies, and ambitions are thwarted at every step, but their inmost thoughts and desires are fed with their own food, be it foul or clean. The "divinity that shapes our ends" is in ourselves; it is our very self. Man is manacled only by himself. Thought and action are the jailers of Fate - they imprison, being base. They are also the angels of Freedom - they liberate, being noble. Not what he wishes and prays for does a man get, but what he justly earns. His wishes and prayers are only gratified and answered when they harmonize with his thoughts and actions.

In the light of this truth, what, then, is the meaning of "fighting against circumstances"? It means that a man is continually revolting against an **effect** without, while all the time he is nourishing and preserving its **cause** in his heart. That cause may take the form of a conscious vice or an unconscious weakness; but whatever it is, it stubbornly retards the efforts of its possessor, and thus calls aloud for remedy.

Men are anxious to improve their circumstances, but are unwilling to improve themselves. They therefore remain bound. The man who does not shrink from self-crucifixion can never fail to accomplish the object upon which his heart is set. This is as true of earthly as of heavenly things. Even the man whose sole object is to acquire wealth must be prepared to make great personal sacrifices before he can accomplish his object; and how much more so he who would realize a strong and well-poised life?

Here is a man who is wretchedly poor. He is extremely anxious that his surroundings and home comforts should be improved. Yet all the time he shirks his work, and considers he is justified in trying to deceive his employer on the ground of the insufficiency of his wages. Such a man does not understand the simplest rudiments of those principles which are the basis of true prosperity. He is not only totally unfitted to rise out of his wretchedness, but is actually attracting to himself a still deeper wretchedness by dwelling in, and acting out, indolent, deceptive, and unmanly thoughts.

Here is a rich man who is the victim of a painful and persistent disease as the result of gluttony. He is willing to give large sums of money to get rid of it, but he will not sacrifice his gluttonous desires. He wants to gratify his taste for rich and unnatural foods and have his health as well. Such a man is totally unfit to have health, because he has not yet learned the first principles of a healthy life.

Here is an employer of labor who adopts crooked measures to avoid paying the regulation wage, and, in the hope of making larger profits, reduces the wages of his work-people. Such a man is altogether unfitted for prosperity. And when he finds himself bankrupt, both as regards reputation and riches, he blames circumstances, not knowing that he is the sole author of his condition.

I have introduced these three cases merely as illustrative of the truth that man is the cause (though nearly always unconsciously) of his circumstances.

That, while aiming at the good end, he is continually frustrating its accomplishment by encouraging thoughts and desires which cannot possibly harmonize with that end. Such cases could be multiplied and varied almost indefinitely, but this is not necessary. The reader can, if he so resolves, trace the action of the laws of thought in his own mind and life, and until this is done, mere external facts cannot serve as a ground of reasoning.

Circumstances, however, are so complicated, thought is so deeply rooted, and the conditions of happiness vary so vastly with individuals, that a man's entire soul condition (although it may be known to himself) cannot be judged by another from the external aspect of his life alone.

A man may be honest in certain directions, yet suffer privations. A man may be dishonest in certain directions, yet acquire wealth. But the conclusion usually formed that the one man fails **because of his particular honesty**, and that the other **prospers because of his particular dishonesty**, is the result of a superficial judgment, which assumes that the dishonest man is almost totally corrupt, and honest man almost entirely virtuous. In the light of a deeper knowledge and wider experience, such judgment is found to be erroneous. The dishonest man may have some admirable virtues which the other does not possess; and the honest man obnoxious vices which are absent in the other. The honest man reaps the good results of his honest thoughts and acts; he also brings upon himself the sufferings which his vices produce. The dishonest man likewise garners his own suffering and happiness.

It is pleasing to human vanity to believe that one suffers because of one's virtue. But not until a man has extirpated every sickly, bitter, and impure thought from his mind, and washed every sinful stain from his soul, can he be in a position to know and declare that his sufferings are the result of his good, and not of his bad qualities. And on the way to that supreme perfection, he will have found working in his mind and life, the Great Law which is absolutely just, and which cannot give good for evil, evil for good. Possessed of such knowledge, he will then know, looking back upon his past ignorance and blindness, that his life is, and always was, justly ordered, and that all his past experiences, good and bad, were the equitable outworking of his evolving, yet unevolved self.

Good thoughts and actions can never produce bad results. Bad thoughts and actions can never produce good results. This is but saying that nothing can come from corn but corn, nothing from nettles but nettles. Men understand this law in the natural world, and work with it. But few understand it in the mental and moral world (though its operation there is just as simple and undeviating), and they, therefore, do not cooperate with it.

Suffering is **always** the effect of wrong thought in some direction. It is an indication that the individual is out of harmony with himself, with the Law of his being. The sole and supreme use of suffering is to purify, to burn out all that is useless and impure. Suffering ceases for him who is pure. There could be not object in burning gold after the dross had been removed, and perfectly pure and enlightened being could not suffer.

The circumstances which a man encounters with suffering are the result of his own mental in-harmony. The circumstances which a man encounters with blessedness, not material possessions, is the measure of right thought. Wretchedness, not lack of material possessions, is the measure of wrong thought. A man may be cursed and rich; he may be blessed and poor. blessedness and riches are only joined together when the riches are rightly and wisely used. And the poor man only descends into wretchedness when he regards his lot as a burden unjustly imposed.

Indigence and indulgence are the two extremes of wretchedness. They are both equally unnatural and the result of mental disorder. A man is not rightly conditioned until he is a happy, healthy, and prosperous being. And happiness, health, and prosperity are the result of a harmonious adjustment of the inner with the outer, of the man with his surroundings.

A man only begins to be a man when he ceases to whine and revile, and commences to search for the hidden justice which regulates his life. And as he adapts his mind to that regulating factor, he ceases to accuse others as the cause of his condition, and builds himself up in strong and noble thoughts. He ceases to kick against circumstances, but begins to **use** them as aids to his more rapid progress, and as a means of discovering the hidden powers and possibilities within himself.

Law, not confusion, is the dominating principle in the universe. Justice, not injustice, is the soul and substance of life. And righteousness, not corruption, is the molding and moving force in the spiritual government of the world. This being so, man has but to right himself to find that the universe is right; and during the process of putting himself right, he will find that as he alters his thoughts toward things and other people, things and other people will alter toward him.

The proof of this truth is in every person, and it therefore admits of easy investigation by systematic introspection and self-analysis. Let a man radically alter his thoughts, and he will be astonished at the rapid transformation it will effect in the material conditions of his life.

Men imagine that thought can be kept secret, but it cannot. It rapidly crystallizes into habit, and habit solidifies into habits of drunkenness and sensuality, which solidify into circumstances of destitution and disease. Impure thoughts of every kind crystallize into enervating and confusing habits, which solidify into distracting and adverse circumstances. Thoughts of fear, doubt, and indecision crystallize into weak, unmanly, and irresolute habits, which solidify into circumstances of failure, indigence, and slavish dependence.

Lazy thoughts crystallize into habits of uncleanliness and dishonesty, which solidify into circumstances of foulness and beggary. Hateful and condemnatory thoughts crystallize into habits of accusation and violence, which solidify into circumstances of injury and persecution. Selfish thoughts of all kinds crystallize into habits of self-seeking, which solidify into circumstances more of less distressing.

On the other hand, beautiful thoughts of all crystallize into habits of grace and kindliness, which solidify into genial and sunny circumstances. Pure thoughts crystallize into habits of temperance and self-control, which solidify into circumstances of repose and peace. Thoughts of courage, self-reliance, and decision crystallize into manly habits, which solidify into circumstances of success, plenty, and freedom.

Energetic thoughts crystallize into habits of cleanliness and industry, which solidify into circumstances of pleasantness. Gentle and forgiving thoughts crystallize into habits of gentleness, which solidify into protective and preservative circumstances. Loving and unselfish thoughts crystallize into habits of self-forgetfulness for others, which solidify into circumstances of sure and abiding prosperity and true riches.

A particular train of thought persisted in, be it good or bad, cannot fail to produce its results on the character and circumstances. A man cannot **directly** choose his circumstances, but he can choose his thoughts, and so indirectly, yet surely, shape his circumstances.

Nature helps every man to the gratification of the thoughts which he most encourages, and opportunities are presented which will most speedily bring to the surface both the good and evil thoughts.

Let a man cease from his sinful thoughts, and all the world will soften toward him, and be ready to help him. Let him put away his weakly and sickly thoughts, and lo! opportunities will spring up on every hand to aid his strong resolves. Let him encourage good thoughts, and no hard fate shall bind him down to wretchedness and shame. The world is your kaleidoscope, and the varying combinations of colors which at every succeeding moment it presents to you are the exquisitely adjusted pictures of your ever-moving thoughts.

"You will be what you will to be;

Let failure find its false content
In that poor word, 'environment,'
But spirit scorns it, and is free.

"It masters time, it conquers space;
It cows that boastful trickster, Chance,
And bids the tyrant Circumstance
Uncrown, and fill a servant's place.

"The human Will, that force unseen,
The offspring of a deathless Soul,
Can hew a way to any goal,
Though walls of granite intervene.

"Be not impatient in delay,
But wait as one who understands;
When spirit rises and commands,
The gods are ready to obey."

Chapter Three

Effect of Thought on Health and the Body

The body is the servant of the mind. It obeys the operations of the mind, whether they be deliberately chosen or automatically expressed. At the bidding of unlawful thoughts the body sinks rapidly into disease and decay; at the command of glad and beautiful thoughts it becomes clothed with youthfulness and beauty.

Disease and health, like circumstances, are rooted in thought. Sickly thoughts will express themselves through a sickly body. Thoughts of fear have been known to kill a man as speedily as a bullet, and they are continually killing thousands of people just as surely though less rapidly. The people who live in fear of disease are the people who get it. Anxiety quickly demoralizes the whole body, and lays it open to the entrance of disease; while impure thoughts, even if not physically indulged, will soon shatter the nervous system.

Strong, pure, and happy thoughts build up the body in vigor and grace. The body is a delicate and plastic instrument, which responds readily to the thoughts by which it is impressed, and habits of thought will produce their own effects, good or bad, upon it.

Men will continue to have impure and poisoned blood so long as they propagate unclean thoughts. Out of a clean heart comes a clean life and a clean body. Out of a defiled mind proceeds a defiled life and corrupt body. Thought is the fountain of action, life and manifestation; make the fountain pure, and all will be pure.

Change of diet will not help a man who will not change his thoughts. When a man makes his thoughts pure, he no longer desires impure food.

If you would perfect your body, guard your mind. If you would renew your body, beautify your mind. Thoughts of malice, envy, disappointment, despondency, rob the body of its health and grace. A sour face does not come by chance; it is made by sour thoughts. Wrinkles that mar are drawn by folly, passion, pride.

I know a woman of ninety-six who has the bright, innocent face of a girl. I know a man well under middle age whose face is drawn into inharmonious contours. The one is the result of a sweet and sunny disposition; the other is the outcome of passion and discontent.

As you cannot have a sweet and wholesome abode unless you admit the air and sunshine freely into your rooms, so a strong body and a bright, happy, or serene countenance can only result from the free admittance into the mind of thoughts of joy and good will and serenity.

On the faces of the aged there are wrinkles made by sympathy, others by strong and pure thought, others are carved by passion. Who cannot distinguish them? With those who have lived righteously, age is calm, peaceful, and softly mellowed, like the setting sun. I have recently seen a philosopher on his deathbed. He was not old except in years. He died as sweetly and peacefully as he had lived.

There is no physician like cheerful thought for dissipating the ills of the body; there is no comforter to compare with good will for dispersing the shadows of grief and sorrow. To live continually in thoughts of ill will, cynicism, suspicion, and envy, is to be confined in a self-made prison hole. But to think well of all, to be cheerful with all, to patiently learn to find the good in all - such unselfish thoughts are the very portals of heaven; and to dwell day to day in thoughts of peace toward every creature will bring abounding peace to their possessor.

Dr. Robert C. Worstell

Chapter Four

Thought and Purpose

Until thought is linked with purpose there is no intelligent accomplishment. With the majority the bark of thought is allowed to "drift" upon the ocean of life. Aimlessness is a vice, and such drifting must not continue for him who would steer clear of catastrophe and destruction.

They who have no central purpose in their life fall an easy prey to worries, fears, troubles, and self-pityings, all of which are indications of weakness, which lead, just as surely as deliberately planned sins (though by a different route), to failure, unhappiness, and loss, for weakness cannot persist in a power-evolving universe.

A man should conceive of a legitimate purpose in his heart, and set out to accomplish it. He should make this purpose the centralizing point of his thoughts. It may take the form of a spiritual ideal, or it may be a worldly object, according to his nature at the time being. But whichever it is, he should steadily focus his thought forces upon the object which he has set before him. He should make this purpose his supreme duty, and should devote himself to its attainment, not allowing his thoughts to wander away into ephemeral fancies, longings, and imaginings. This is the royal road to self-control and true concentration of thought. Even if he fails again and again to accomplish his purpose (as he necessarily must until weakness is overcome), **the strength of character gained** will be the measure of **his true** success, and this will form a new starting point for future power and triumph.

Those who are not prepared for the apprehension of a **great** purpose, should fix the thoughts upon the faultless performance of their duty, no matter how insignificant their task may appear. Only in this way can the thoughts be gathered and focused, and resolution and energy be developed, which being done, there is nothing which may not be accomplished.

The weakest soul, knowing its own weakness, and believing this truth – **that strength can only be developed by effort and practice**, will at once begin to exert itself, and adding effort to effort, patience to patience, and strength to strength, will never cease to develop, and will at last grow divinely strong.

As the physically weak man can make himself strong by careful and patient training, so the man of weak thoughts can make them strong by exercising himself in right thinking.

To put away aimlessness and weakness, and to begin to think with purpose, is to enter the ranks of those strong ones who only recognize failure as one of the pathways to attainment; who make all conditions serve them, and who think strongly, attempt fearlessly, and accomplish masterfully.

Having conceived of his purpose, a man should mentally mark out a **straight** pathway to its achievement, looking neither to the right nor to the left. Doubts and fears should be rigorously excluded; they are disintegrating elements which break up the straight line of effort, rendering it crooked, ineffectual, useless. Thoughts of doubt and fear never accomplish anything, and never can. They always lead to failure. Purpose, energy, power to do, and all strong thoughts cease when doubt and fear creep in.

The will to do springs from the knowledge that we **can** do. Doubt and fear are the great enemies of knowledge, and he who encourages them, who does not slay them, thwarts himself at every step.

He who has conquered doubt and fear has conquered failure. His every thought is allied with power, and all difficulties are bravely met and wisely overcome. His purposes are seasonably planted, and they bloom and bring forth fruit which does not fall prematurely to the ground.

Thought allied fearlessly to purpose becomes creative force. He who **knows** this is ready to become something higher and stronger than a mere bundle of wavering thoughts and fluctuating sensations.

He who **does** this has become the conscious and intelligent wielder of his mental powers.

Chapter Five

The Thought-Factor in Achievement

All that a man achieves and all that he fails to achieve is the direct result of his own thoughts. In a justly ordered universe, where loss of equipoise would mean total destruction, individual responsibility must be absolute. A man's weakness and strength, purity and impurity, are his own, and not another man's. They are brought about by himself, and not by another; and they can only be altered by himself, never by another. His condition is also his own, and not another man's. His suffering and his happiness are evolved from within. As he thinks, so he is; as he continues to think, so he remains.

A strong man cannot help a weaker unless the weaker is **willing** to be helped, and even then the weak man must become strong of himself. He must, by his own efforts, develop the strength which he admires in another. None but himself can alter his condition.

It has been usual for men to think and to say, "Many men are slaves because one is an oppressor; let us hate the oppressor." Now, however, there is among an increasing few a tendency to reverse this judgment, and to say, "One man is an oppressor because many are slaves; let us despise the slaves." The truth is that oppressor and slave are cooperators in ignorance, and, while seeming to afflict each other, are in reality afflicting themselves. A perfect Knowledge perceives the action of law in the weakness of the oppressed and the misapplied power of the oppressor. A perfect Love, seeing the suffering which both states entail, condemns neither. A perfect Compassion embraces both oppressor and oppressed.

He who has conquered weakness, and has put away all selfish thoughts, belongs neither to oppressor nor oppressed. He is free.

A man can only rise, conquer, and achieve by lifting up his thoughts. He can only remain weak, and abject, and miserable by refusing to lift up his thoughts.

Before a man can achieve anything, even in worldly things, he must lift his thoughts above slavish animal indulgence. He may not, in order to succeed, give up all animality and selfishness, by any means; but a portion of it must, at least, be sacrificed. A man whose first thought is bestial indulgence could neither think clearly nor plan methodically. He could not find and develop his latent resources, and would fail in any undertaking. Not having commenced manfully to control his thoughts, he is not in a position to control affairs and to adopt serious responsibilities. He is not fit to act independently and stand alone, but he is limited only by the thoughts which he chooses.

There can be no progress, no achievement without sacrifice. A man's worldly success will be in the measure that he sacrifices his confused animal thoughts, and fixes his mind on the development of his plans, and the strengthening of his resolution and self reliance. And the higher he lifts his thoughts, the more manly, upright, and righteous he becomes, the greater will be his success, the more blessed an enduring will be his achievements.

The universe does not favor the greedy, the dishonest, the vicious, although on the mere surface it may sometimes appear to do so; it helps the honest, the magnanimous, the virtuous. All the great Teachers of the ages have declared this in varying forms, and to prove and know it a man has but to persist in making himself more and more virtuous by lifting up his thoughts.

Intellectual achievements are the result of thought consecrated to the search for knowledge, or for the beautiful and true in life and nature. Such achievements may be sometimes connected with vanity and ambition but they are not the outcome of those characteristics. They are the natural outgrowth of long an arduous effort, and of pure and unselfish thoughts.

Spiritual achievements are the consummation of holy aspirations. He who lives constantly in the conception of noble and lofty thoughts, who dwells upon all that is pure and unselfish, will, as surely as the sun reaches its zenith and the moon its full, become wise and noble in character, and rise into a position of influence and blessedness.

Achievement, of whatever kind, is the crown of effort, the diadem of thought. By the aid of self-control, resolution, purity, righteousness, and well-directed thought a man ascends. By the aid of animality, indolence, impurity, corruption, and confusion of thought a man descends.

A man may rise to high success in the world, and even to lofty altitudes in the spiritual realm, and again descend into weakness and wretchedness by allowing arrogant, selfish, and corrupt thoughts to take possession of him.

Victories attained by right thought can only be maintained by watchfulness. Many give way when success is assured, and rapidly fall back into failure.

All achievements, whether in the business, intellectual, or spiritual world, are the result of definitely directed thought, are governed by the same law and are of the same method; the only difference lies in **the object of attainment**.

He who would accomplish little must sacrifice little. He who would achieve much must sacrifice much. He who would attain highly must sacrifice greatly.

Chapter Six

Visions and Ideals

The dreamers are the saviors of the world. As the visible world is sustained by the invisible, so men, through all their trials and sins and sordid vocations, are nourished by the beautiful visions of their solitary dreamers. Humanity cannot forget its dreamers. It cannot let their ideals fade and die. It lives in them. It knows them in the **realities** which it shall one day see and know.

Composer, sculptor, painter, poet, prophet, sage, these are the makers of the afterworld, the architects of heaven. The world is beautiful because they have lived; without them, laboring humanity would perish.

He who cherishes a beautiful vision, a lofty ideal in his heart, will one day realize it. Columbus cherished a vision of another world, and he discovered it. Copernicus fostered the vision of a multiplicity of worlds and a wider universe, and he revealed it. Buddha beheld the vision of a spiritual world of stainless beauty and perfect peace, and he entered into it.

Cherish your visions. Cherish your ideals. Cherish the music that stirs in your heart, the beauty that forms in your mind, the loveliness that drapes your purest thoughts, for out of them will grow all delightful conditions, all heavenly environment; of these, if you but remain true to them, your world will at last be built.

To desire is to obtain; to aspire is to achieve. Shall man's basest desires receive the fullest measure of gratification, and his purest aspirations starve for lack of sustenance? Such is not the Law. Such a condition of things can never obtain - "Ask and receive."

Dream lofty dreams, and as you dream, so shall you become. Your Vision is the promise of what you shall one day be. Your Ideal is the prophecy of what you shall at last unveil.

The greatest achievement was at first and for a time a dream. The oak sleeps in the acorn; the bird waits in the egg; and in the highest vision of the soul a waking angel stirs. Dreams are the seedlings of realities.

Your circumstances may be uncongenial, but they shall not long remain so if you but perceive an Ideal and strive to reach it. You cannot travel **within** and stand still **without**. Here is a youth hard pressed by poverty and labor; confined long hours in an unhealthy workshop; unschooled, and lacking all the arts of refinement. But he dreams of better things. He thinks of intelligence, of refinement, of grace and beauty. He conceives of, mentally builds up, an ideal condition of life. The vision of the wider liberty and a larger scope takes possession of him; unrest urges him to action, and he utilizes all his spare time and means, small though they are, to the development of his latent powers and resources.

Very soon so altered has his mind become that the workshop can no longer hold him. It has become so out of harmony with his mentality that it falls out of his life as a garment is cast aside, and with the growth of opportunities which fit the scope of his expanding powers, he passes out of it forever.

Years later we see this youth as a full-grown man. We find him a master of certain forces of the mind which he wields with world-wide influence and almost unequaled power. In his hands he holds the cords of gigantic responsibilities. He speaks, and lo! lives are changed. Men and women hang upon his words and re-mold their characters, and, sun-like, he becomes the fixed and luminous center around which innumerable destinies revolve. He has realized the Vision of his youth. He has become one with his Ideal.

And you, too, youthful reader, will realize the Vision (not the idle wish) of your heart, be it base or beautiful, or a mixture of both, for you will always gravitate toward that which you secretly most love. Into your hands will be placed the exact results of your own thoughts; you will receive that which you earn, no more, no less. Whatever your present environment may be, you will fall, remain, or rise with your thoughts, your Vision, your Ideal. You will become as small as your controlling desire; as great as your dominant aspiration.

In the beautiful words of Stanton Kirkham Dave, "You may be keeping accounts, and presently you shall walk out of the door that for so long has seemed to you the barrier of your ideals, and shall find yourself before an audience - the pen still behind your ear, the ink stains on your fingers - and then and there shall pour out the torrent of your inspiration. You may be driving sheep, and you shall wander to the city - bucolic and open mouthed; shall wander under the intrepid guidance of the spirit into the studio of the master, and after a time he shall say, 'I have nothing more to teach you.' And now you have become the master, who did so recently dream of great things while driving sheep. You shall lay down the saw and the plane to take upon yourself the regeneration of the world."

The thoughtless, the ignorant, and the indolent, seeing only the apparent effects of things and not the things themselves, talk of luck, of fortune, and chance. See a man grow rich, they say, "How lucky he is!" Observing another become intellectual, they exclaim, "How highly favored he is!" And noting the saintly character and wide influence of another, the remark, "How chance aids him at every turn!"

They do not see the trials and failures and struggles which these men have voluntarily encountered in order to gain their experience. They have no knowledge of the sacrifices they have made, of the undaunted efforts they have put forth, of the faith they have exercised, that they might overcome the apparently insurmountable, and realize the Vision of their heart. They do not know the darkness and the heartaches; they only see the light and joy, and call it "luck"; do not see the long and arduous journey, but only behold the pleasant goal, and call it "good fortune"; do not understand the process, but only perceive the result, and call it "chance."

In all human affairs there are **efforts**, and there are **results**, and the strength of the effort is the measure of the result. Chance is not. "Gifts," powers, material, intellectual, and spiritual possessions are the fruits of effort. They are thoughts completed, objects accomplished, visions realized.

The vision that you glorify in your mind, the Ideal that you enthrone in your heart – this you will build your life by, this you will become.

Chapter Seven

Serenity

Calmness of mind is one of the beautiful jewels of wisdom. It is the result of long and patient effort in self-control. Its presence is an indication of ripened experience, and of a more than ordinary knowledge of the laws and operations of thought.

A man becomes calm in the measure that he understands himself as a thought-evolved being, for such knowledge necessitates the understanding of others as the result of thought. As he develops a right understanding, and sees more and more clearly the internal relations of things by the action of cause and effect, he ceases to fuss and fume and worry and grieve, and remains poised, steadfast, serene.

The calm man, having learned how to govern himself, knows how to adapt himself to others; and they, in turn, reverence his spiritual strength, and feel that they can learn of him and rely upon him. The more tranquil a man becomes, the greater is his success, his influence, his power for good. Even the ordinary trader will find his business prosperity increase as he develops a greater self-control and equanimity, for people will always prefer to deal with a man whose demeanor is strongly equable.

The strong calm man is always loved and revered. He is like a shade-giving tree in a thirsty land, or a sheltering rock in a storm. Who does not love a tranquil heart, a sweet-tempered, balanced life? It does not matter whether it rains or shines, or what changes come to those possessing these blessings, for they are always sweet, serene, and calm. That exquisite poise of character which we call serenity is the last lesson culture; it is the flowering of life, the fruitage of the soul. It is precious as wisdom, more to be desired than gold -yea, than even fine gold. How insignificant mere money-seeking looks in comparison with a serene life - a life that dwells in the ocean of Truth, beneath the waves, beyond the reach of tempests, in the Eternal Calm!

How many people we know who sour their lives, who ruin all that is sweet and beautiful by explosive tempers, who destroy their poise of character,and make bad blood! It is a question whether the great majority of people do not ruin their lives and mar their happiness by lack of self-control. How few people we meet in life who are well-balanced, who have that exquisite poise which is characteristic of the finished character!

Yes, humanity surges with uncontrolled passion, is tumultuous with ungoverned grief, is blown about by anxiety and doubt. Only the wise man, only he whose thoughts are controlled and purified, makes the winds and the storms of the soul obey him.

Tempest-tossed souls, wherever ye may be, under whatsoever conditions ye may live, know this - in the ocean of life the isles of Blessedness are smiling, and sunny shore of your ideal awaits your coming. Keep your hand firmly upon the helm of thought. In the bark of your soul reclines the commanding Master; He does but sleep; wake Him. Self-control is strength; Right Thought is mastery; Calmness is power. Say unto your heart, "Peace, be still!"

Dr. Robert C. Worstell

A Summary of <u>The Science of Getting Rich</u>

The final chapter from the book of the same name, originally published 1920.

THERE IS A THINKING STUFF FROM WHICH ALL THINGS ARE MADE, and which, in its original state, permeates, penetrates, and fills the inter-spaces of the universe.

A thought in this substance produces the thing that is imaged by the thought.

A person can form things in his thought, and by impressing his thought upon formless substance can cause the thing he thinks about to be created.

In order to do this, a person must pass from the competitive to the creative mind. Otherwise he cannot be in harmony with formless intelligence, which is always creative and never competitive in spirit.

A person may come into full harmony with the formless substance by entertaining a lively and sincere gratitude for the blessings it bestows upon him. Gratitude unifies the mind of man with the intelligence of substance, so that man's thoughts are received by the formless. A person can remain upon the creative plane only by uniting himself with the formless intelligence through a deep and continuous feeling of gratitude.

A person must form a clear and definite mental image of the things he wishes to have, to do, or to become, and he must hold this mental image in his thoughts, while being deeply grateful to the supreme that all his desires are granted to him. The person who wishes to get rich must spend his leisure hours in contemplating his vision, and in earnest thanksgiving that the reality is being given to him. Too much stress cannot be laid on the importance of frequent contemplation of the mental image, coupled with unwavering faith and devout gratitude. This is the process by which the impression is given to the formless and the creative forces set in motion.

The creative energy works through the established channels of natural growth, and of the industrial and social order. All that is included in his mental image will surely be brought to the person who follows the instructions given above, and whose faith does not waver. What he wants will come to him through the ways of established trade and commerce.

In order to receive his own when it is ready to come to him, a person must be in action in a way that causes him to more than fill his present place. He must keep in mind the purpose to get rich through realization of his mental image. And he must do, every day, all that can be done that day, taking care to do each act in a successful manner. He must give to every person a use value in excess of the cash value he receives, so that each transaction makes for more life, and he must hold the advancing thought so that the impression of increase will be communicated to all with whom he comes into contact.

The men and women who practice the foregoing instructions will certainly get rich, and the riches they receive will be in exact proportion to the definiteness of their vision, the fixity of their purpose, the steadiness of their faith, and the depth of their gratitude.

Master Key System
Study Questions with Answers

by Charles Haanel

excerpted from the book of the same name,
which was originally published in 1912.

1. What is the world without in its relation to the world within?
    The world without is a reflection of the world within.

2. Upon what does all possession depend?
    All possession is based on consciousness.

3. How is the individual related to the objective world?
    The individual is related to the objective world by the objective mind; the brain is the organ of this mind.

4. How is he related to the Universal Mind?
    He is related to the Universal Mind by the subconscious mind; the Solar Plexus is the organ of this mind.

5. What is the Universal Mind?
    The Universal Mind is the life principle of every atom which is in existence.

6. How can the Individual act on the Universal?
>   The ability of the individual to think is his ability to act upon the Universal and bring it into manifestation.

7. What is the result of this action and interaction?
>   The result of this action and interaction is cause and effect; every thought is a cause and every condition an effect.

8. How are harmonious and desirable conditions secured?
>   Harmonious and desirable conditions are obtained by right thinking.

9. What is the cause of all discord, inharmony, lack and limitation?
>   Discord, inharmony, lack and limitation are the result of wrong thinking.

10. What is the source of all powers?
>   The source of all power is the world within, the Universal Fountain of Supply, the Infinite Energy of which each individual is an outlet.

11. What are the two modes of mental activity?
>   Conscious and subconscious.

12. Upon what do ease and perfection depend?

   Ease and perfection depend entirely upon the degree in which we cease to depend upon the conscious mind.

13. What is the value of the subconscious?

   It is enormous; it guides us, warns us, it controls the vital processes and is the seat of memory.

14. What are some of the functions of the conscious mind?

   It has the faculty of discrimination; it has the power of reasoning; it is the seat of the will and may impress the subconscious.

15. How has the distinction between the conscious and subconscious been expressed?

   "Conscious mind is reasoning will. Subconscious mind is instinctive desire, the result of past reasoning will."

16. What method is necessary in order to impress the subconscious?

   Mentally state what is wanted.

17. What will be the result?

   If the desire is in harmony with the forward movement of the great Whole, forces will be set in motion which will bring about the result.

18. What is the result of the operation of this law?
    Our environment reflects conditions corresponding to the predominant mental attitude which we entertain.

19. What names has been given to this law?
    The Law of Attraction.

20. How is the law stated?
    Thought is a creative energy, and will automatically correlate with is object and bring it into manifestation.

21. What system of nerves is the organ of the Conscious Mind?
    The Cerebro-spinal.

22. What system of nerves is the organ of the subconscious mind?
    The sympathetic.

23. What is the central point of distribution for energy which the body is constantly generating?
    The solar plexus.

24. How may this distribution be interrupted?
    By resistant, critical, discordant thoughts, but especially fear.

25. What is the result of such interruption?
> Every ill with which the human race is afflicted.

26. How may this energy be controlled and directed?
> By conscious thought.

27. How may fear be completely eliminated?
> By an understanding and recognition of the true source of all power.

28. What determines the experiences with which we meet in life?
> Our predominant mental attitude.

29. How may we awake the solar plexus?
> Mentally concentrate upon the condition which we desire to see manifested in our lives.

30. What is the creative principle of the Universe?
> The Universal Mind.

31. What is thought?
> Thought is spiritual energy.

32. How is it carried?
> By the law of vibration.

33. How is it given vitality?
    By the law of love.

34. How does it take form?
    By the law of growth.

35. What is the secret of its creative power?
    It is a spiritual activity.

36. How may we develop the faith, courage, and enthusiasm which will result in accomplishment?
    By a recognition of our spiritual nature.

37. What is the secret of Power?
    Service.

38. Why is this so?
    Because we get what we give.

39. What is the Silence?
    A physical stillness.

40. Of what value is it?

> It is the first step to self-control, self-mastery.

41. What proportion of our mental life is subconscious?

> At least ninety per cent.

42. Is this vast mental storehouse generally utilized?

> No.

43. Why not?

> Few understand or appreciate the fact that it is an activity which they may consciously direct.

44. Where has the conscious mind received its governing tendencies?

> From heredity -- which means that it is the result of all the environments of all past generations.

45. What is the law of attraction bringing to us?

> Our "Own."

46. What is our "Own"?

> What we inherently are, and is the result of our past thinking, both conscious and subconscious.

47. Of what is the material with which we construct our mental home composed?

The thoughts which we entertain.

48. What is the Secret of Power?

A recognition of the omnipresence of omnipotence.

49. Where does it originate?

All life and all power is from within.

50. Upon what is the possession of power contingent?

Upon a proper use of the power already in our possession.

51. What are some of the effects which can be produced by electricity?

Heat, light, power, music.

52. Upon what do these various effects depend?

Upon the mechanism to which electricity is attached.

53. What is the result of the action and interaction of the individual mind upon the Universal?

The conditions and experiences with which we meet.

54. How may these conditions be changed?

> By changing the mechanism by which the Universal is differentiated in form.

55. What is this mechanism?

> The brain.

56. How may it be changed?

> By the process we call thinking. Thoughts produce brain cells, and these cells respond to the corresponding thought in the Universal.

57. Of what value is the power of concentration?

> It is the very highest personal accomplishment which can be acquired, and the distinguishing characteristic of every successful man or woman.

58. How may it be acquired?

> By faithfully practicing the exercises in this System.

59. Why is this so important?

> Because it will enable us to control our thoughts, and since thoughts are causes conditions must be effects; if we can control the cause we can also control the effect.

60. What is changing conditions and multiplying results in the objective world?

    Men are learning the basic methods of constructive thinking.

61. What is visualization?

    The process of making mental pictures.

62. What is the result of this method of thought?

    By holding the image or picture in mind, we can gradually but surely bring the thing nearer to us. We can be what we will to be.

63. What is Idealization?

    It is a process of visualizing or idealizing the plans which will eventually materialize in our objective world.

64. Why are clearness and accuracy necessary?

    Because "seeing" creates "feeling" and "feeling" creates "being." First the mental, then the emotional, then the illimitable possibilities of achievement.

65. How are they obtained?

    Each repeated action renders the image more accurate than the former one.

66. How is the material for the construction of your mental image secured?

   By millions of mental workers. Brain cells they are called.

67. How are the necessary conditions for bringing about the materialization of your ideal in the objective world secured?

   By the Law of Attraction. The natural law by which all conditions and experiences are brought about.

68. What three steps are necessary in order to bring this law into operation?

   Earnest Desire, Confident Expectation, Firm Demand.

69. Why do many fail?

   Because they concentrate on loss, disease and disaster. The law is operating perfectly; the things they fear are coming upon them.

70. What is the alternative?

   Concentrate on the ideals which you desire to see manifested in your life.

71. What is the imagination?

   A form of constructive thought. The light by which we penetrate new worlds of thought and experience. The mighty instrument by which every inventor or discoverer opened the way from precedent to experience.

72. What is the result of imagination?

    The cultivation of the imagination leads to the development of the ideal out of which your future will emerge.

73. How may it be cultivated?

    By exercise; it must be supplied with nourishment or it cannot live.

74. How does imagination differ from day dreaming?

    Day dreaming is a form of mental dissipation, while imagination is a form of constructive thought which must precede every constructive action.

75. What are mistakes?

    The result of ignorance.

76. What is knowledge?

    The result of man's ability to think.

77. What is the power with which successful men build?

    Mind is the very moving force with which they secure the persons and circumstances necessary to complete their plans.

78. What pre-determines the result?
> The ideal held steadily in mind attracts the necessary conditions for its fulfillment.

79. What is the result of a keen analytical observation?
> The development of imagination, insight, perception and sagacity.

80. To what do these lead?
> Opulence and harmony.

81. What is the imperative condition of all well-being?
> Well doing.

82. What is the condition precedent to every right action?
> Right thinking.

83. What is the underlying condition necessary in every business transaction or social relation?
> To know the Truth.

84. What is the result of a knowledge of the Truth?
> We can readily predict the result of any action that is based upon a true premise.

85. What is the result of any action based upon a false premise?
> We can form no conception of the results which may ensue.

86. How may we know the Truth?
> By a realization of the fact that Truth is the vital principle of the Universe and is therefore omnipresent.

87. What is the nature of Truth?
> It is spiritual.

88. What is the secret of the solution to every problem?
> To apply spiritual Truth.

89. What is the advantage of spiritual methods?
> They are always available.

90. What are the necessary requirements?
> A recognition of the omnipotence of spiritual power and a desire to become the recipient of its beneficent effects.

91. What is Wealth?
> Wealth is the offspring of power.

92. Of what value are possessions?

> Possessions are of value only as they confer power.

93. Of what value is a knowledge of cause and effect?

> It enables men to plan courageously and execute fearlessly.

94. How does life originate in the inorganic world?

> Only by the introduction of some living form. There is no other way.

95. What is the connecting link between the finite and the Infinite?

> Thought is the connecting link.

96. Why is that so?

> Because the Universal can manifest only through the individual.

97. Upon what does causation depend?

> Upon polarity; a circuit must be formed; the Universal is the positive side of the battery of life, the individual is the negative, and thought forms the circuit.

98. Why do many fail to secure harmonious conditions?

> They do not understand the law; there is no polarity; they have not formed the circuit.

99. What is the remedy?

> A conscious recognition of the law of attraction with the intention of bring it into existence for a definite purpose.

100. What will be the result?

> Thought will correlate with its object and bring it into manifestation, because thought is a product of the spiritual man, and spirit is the creative Principle of the Universe.

101. What is inductive reasoning?

> The process of the objective mind by which we compare a number of separate instances with each other until we see the common factor which gives rise to them all.

102. What has this method of studying accomplished?

> It has resulted in the discovery of a reign of law which has marked an epoch in human progress.

103. What is it that guides and determines action?

> It is need, want and desire which in the largest sense induce, guide and determine action.

104. What is the formula for the unerring solution of every individual problem?

> We are to believe that our desire has already been fulfilled; its accomplishment will then follow.

105. What great Teachers advocated it?
>   Jesus, Plato, Swedenborg.

106. What is the result of this thought process?
>   We are thinking on the plane of the absolute and planting a seed, which if left undisturbed will germinate into fruition.

107. Why is it scientifically exact?
>   Because it is Natural Law.

108. What is Faith?
>   "Faith is the substance of things hoped for, the evidence of things unseen."

109. What is the Law of Attraction?
>   The Law by which Faith is brought into manifestation.

110. What importance do you attach to an understanding of this law?
>   It has eliminated the elements of uncertainty and caprice from men's lives and substituted law, reason, and certitude.

111. How may any purpose in life be best accomplished?
>   Through a scientific understanding of the spiritual nature of thought.

112. What three steps are absolutely essential?
> The knowledge of our power, the courage to dare, the faith to do.

113. How is the practical working knowledge secured?
> By an understanding of Natural laws.

114. What is the reward of an understanding of these laws?
> A conscious realization of our ability to adjust ourselves to Divine and unchanging principle.

115. What will indicate the degree of success with which we meet?
> The degree in which we realize that we cannot change the Infinite but must cooperate with it.

116. What is the principle which gives thought its dynamic power?
> The Law of Attraction which rests on vibration, which in turn rests upon the law of love. Thought impregnated with love becomes invincible.

117. Why is this law irresistible?
> Because it is a Natural law. All Natural laws are irresistible and unchangeable and act with mathematical exactitude. There is no deviation or variation.

118. Why then does it sometimes seem to be difficult to find the solution to our problems in life?

For the same reason that it is sometimes difficult to find the correct solution to a difficult mathematical problem. The operator is uninformed or inexperienced.

119. Why is it impossible for the mind to grasp an entirely new idea?

We have no corresponding vibratory brain cell capable of receiving the idea.

120. How is wisdom secured?

By concentration; it is an unfoldment; it comes from within.

121. What is the method by which natural philosophers obtain and apply their knowledge?

To observe individual facts carefully, patiently, accurately, with all the instruments and resources at their command, before venturing upon a statement of general laws.

122. How may we be certain that this method is correct?

By not permitting a tyrannical prejudice to neglect or mutilate unwelcome facts.

123. What class of facts are esteemed most highly?
> Those which cannot be accounted for by the usual daily observation of life.

124. Upon what is this principle founded?
> Upon reason and experience.

125. What does it destroy?
> Superstition, precedent and conventionality.

126. How have these laws been discovered?
> By a generalization of facts which are uncommon, rare, strange and form the exception.

127. How may we account for much of the strange and heretofore unexplainable phenomena which is constantly taking place?
> By the creative power of thought.

128. Why is this so?
> Because when we learn of a fact we can be sure that it is the result of a certain definite cause and that this cause will operate with invariable precision.

129. What is the result of this knowledge?

> It will explain the cause of every possible condition, whether physical, mental or spiritual.

130. How will our best interest be conserved?

> By a recognition of the fact that a knowledge of the creative nature of thought puts us in touch with Infinite power.

131. What is the source of all Wisdom, Power and Intelligence?

> The Universal Mind.

132. Where do all motion, light, heat and color have their origin?

> In the Universal Energy, which is one manifestation of the Universal Mind.

133. Where does the creative power of thought originate?

> In the Universal Mind.

134. What is thought?

> Mind in motion.

135. How is the Universal differentiated in form?

> The individual is the means by which the Universal produces the various combinations which result in formation of phenomena.

136. How is this accomplished?
> The power of the individual to think is his ability to act upon the Universal and bring it into manifestation.

137. What is the first form which the Universal takes so far as we know? Electrons, which fill all space.

138. Where do all things have their origin?
> In mind.

139. What is the result of a change of thought?
> A change in conditions.

140. What is the result of a harmonious mental attitude?
> Harmonious conditions in life. Thought, immaterial though it may be, is the matrix that shapes the issues of life.

141. What determines the degree of harmony which we attain?
> Our ability to appropriate what we require for our growth from each experience.

142. What do difficulties and obstacles indicate?
> That they are necessary for our wisdom and spiritual growth.

143. How may these difficulties be avoided?

> By a conscious understanding of and cooperation with Natural laws.

144. What is the principle by which thought manifests itself in form?
> The Law of Attraction.

145. How is the necessary material secured by which the growth, development and maturity of the idea take form?
> The law of love, which is the creative principle of the Universe, imparts vitality to the thought, and the law of attraction brings the necessary substance by the law of growth.

146. How are desirable conditions secured? By entertaining desirable thoughts only.

147. How are undesirable conditions brought about?
> By thinking, discussing and visualizing conditions of lack, limitation, disease, inharmony and discord of every kind. This mental photography of erroneous conceptions is taken up by the subconscious and the law of attraction will inevitable crystallize it into objective form. That we reap what we sow is scientifically exact.

148. How can we overcome every kind of fear, lack. limitation, poverty and discord?

By substituting principle for error.

149. How may we recognize principle?

By a conscious realization of the fact that Truth invariably destroys error. We do not have to laboriously shovel the darkness out; all that is necessary is to turn on the light. The same principle applies to every form of negative thought.

150. What is the value of Insight?

It enables us to understand the value of making application of the knowledge which we gain. Many seem to think that knowledge will automatically apply itself, which is by no means true.

151. Upon what does wealth depend?

Upon an understanding of the creative nature of thought.

152. Upon what does its true value consist?

Upon its exchange value.

153. Upon what does success depend?

Upon spiritual power.

154. Upon what does this power depend?

>Upon use; use determines its existence.

155. How may we take our fate out of the hands of chance?

>By consciously realizing the conditions which we desire to see manifested in our lives.

156. What then is the great business of life?

>Thinking.

157. Why is this so?

>Because thought is spiritual and therefore creative. To consciously control thought is therefore to control circumstances, conditions, environment and destiny.

158. What is the source of all evil?

>Destructive thinking.

159. What is the source of all good?

>Scientific correct thinking.

160. What is scientific thinking?

>A recognition of the creative nature of spiritual energy and our ability to control it.

161. What is the true method of concentration?
> To become so identified wit the object of your thought that you are conscious of nothing else.

162. What is the result of this method of concentration?
> Invisible forces are set in motion which irresistibly bring about conditions in correspondence with your thought.

163. What is the controlling factor in this method of thought?
> Spiritual Truth.

164. Why is this so?
> Because the nature of our desire must be in harmony with Natural Law.

165. What is the practical value of this method of concentration?
> Thought is transmuted into character, and character is the magnet which creates the environment of the individual.

166. What is the controlling factor in every commercial pursuit?
> The mental element.

167. Why is this so?
> Because Mind is the ruler and creator of all form and all events occurring in form.

168. How does concentration operate?

By the development of the powers of perception, wisdom, intuition, and sagacity.

169. Why is intuition superior to reason?

Because it does not depend upon experience or memory and frequently brings about the solution to our problems by methods concerning which we are in entire ignorance.

170. What is the result of pursuing the symbol of the reality?

They frequently turn to ashes just as we overtake them, because the symbol is only the outward form of the spiritual activity within, therefore unless we can possess the spiritual reality, the form disappears.

171. How is the difference in individual lives measured?

By the degree of intelligence which they manifest.

172. What is the law by which the individual may control other forms of intelligence?

A recognition of the self as an individualization of the Universal Intelligence.

173. Where does the creative power originate?

In the Universal.

174. How does the Universal create form?
>By means of the individual.

175. What is the connecting link between the individual and the Universal?
>Thought.

176. What is the principle by which the means of existence is carried into effect?
>The Law of Love.

177. How is this principle brought into expression?
>By the law of growth.

178. Upon what condition does the law of growth depend?
>Upon reciprocal action. The individual is complete at all times and this makes it possible to receive only as we give.

179. What is it that we give?
>Thought.

180. What do we receive?
>Thought, which is substance in equilibrium and which is constantly being differentiated in form by what we think.

181. How are extremes placed in contrast?

>They are designated by distinctive names, such as inside and outside, top and bottom, light and dark, good and bad.

182. Are these separate entities?

>No, they are parts or aspects of one Whole.

183. What is the one creative Principle in the physical, mental and spiritual world?

>The Universal Mind, or the Eternal Energy from which all things proceed.

184. How are we related to this creative Principle?

>By our ability to think.

185. How does this creative Principle become operative?

>Thought is the seed, which results in action and action results in form.

186. Upon what does form depend?

>Upon the rate of vibration.

187. How may the rate of vibration be changed?

>By mental action.

188. Upon what does mental action depend?

> Upon polarity, action and reaction, between the individual and the Universal.

189. Does the creative energy originate in the individual or the Universal? In the Universal, but the Universal can manifest only through the individual.

190. Why is the individual necessary?

> Because the Universal is static, and requires energy to start it in motion. This is furnished by food which is converted into energy, which in turn enables the individual to think. When the individual stops eating he stops thinking; then he no longer acts upon the Universal; there is consequently no longer any action or reaction; the Universal is then only pure mind in static form -- mind at rest.

191. Upon what condition does power depend?

> Upon recognition and use.

192. What is recognition?

> Consciousness.

193. How do we become conscious of power?

> By thinking.

194. What then is the true business of life?
>   Correct scientific thinking.

195. What is correct scientific thinking?
>   The ability to adjust our thought processes to the will of the Universal. In other words, to cooperate with Natural laws.

196. How is this accomplished?
>   By securing a perfect understanding of the principles, forces, methods and combinations of mind.

197. What is this Universal Mind?
>   The basic fact of all existence.

198. What is the cause of all lack, limitation, disease and discord?
>   It is due to the operation of exactly the same law, the law operates relentlessly and is continually bringing about conditions in correspondence with the thought which originated or created them.

199. What is inspiration?
>   The art of realizing the omnipresence of Omniscience.

200. Upon what does the conditions with which we meet depend?
> Upon the quality of our thought. Because what we do depends upon what we are and what we are depends upon what we think.

201. What is the real secret of power?
> The consciousness of power, because whatever we become conscious of, is invariably manifested in the objective world, is brought forth into tangible expression.

202. What is the source of this power?
> The Universal Mind, from which all things proceed, and which is one and indivisible.

203. How is this power being manifested?
> Through the individual, each individual is a channel whereby this energy is being differentiated in form.

204. How may we connect with this Omnipotence?
> Our ability to think is our ability to act on this Universal Energy, and what we think is what is produced or created in the objective world.

205. What is the result of this discovery?
> The result is nothing less than marvelous, it opens unprecedented and limitless opportunity.

206. How, then, may we eliminate imperfect conditions?
> By becoming conscious of our Unity with the source of all power.

207. What is one of the distinctive characteristics of the Master Mind?
> He thinks big thoughts, he holds ideas large enough to counteract and destroy all petty and annoying obstacles.

208. How do experiences come to us?
> Through the law of attraction.

209. How is this law brought into operation?
> By our predominant mental attitude.

210. What is the issue between the old regime and the new?
> A question of conviction as to the nature of the Universe. The old regime is trying to cling to the fatalistic doctrine of Divine election. The new regime recognizes the divinity of the individual, the democracy of humanity.

211. How may sickness be eliminated?
> By placing ourselves in harmony with Natural Law which is Omnipotent.

212. What is the process?

> A realization that man is a spiritual being and that this spirit must necessarily be perfect.

213. What is the result?

> A conscious recognition of this perfection - first intellectually, then emotionally - brings about a manifestation of this perfection.

214. Why is this so?

> Because thought is spiritual and therefore creative and correlates with its object and brings it into manifestation.

215. What Natural Law is brought into operation?

> The Law of Vibration.

216. Why does this govern?

> Because a higher rate of vibration governs, modifies, controls, changes, or destroys a lower rate of vibration.

217. Is this system of mental therapeutics generally recognized?

> Yes, there are literally millions of people in this country who make use of it in one form or another (and obviously many more world-wide).

218. What is the result of this system of thought?

>   For the first time in the world's history every man's highest reasoning faculty can be satisfied by a demonstrable truth which is now fast flooding the world.

219. Is this system applicable to other forms of supply?

>   It will meet every human requirement or necessity.

220. Is this system scientific or religious?

>   Both. True science and true religion are twin sisters, where one goes, the other necessarily follows.

221. What is the first law of success?

>   Service.

222. How may we be of the most service?

>   Have an open mind; be interested in the race rather than the goal, in the pursuit rather than possession.

223. What is the result of a selfish thought?

>   It contains the germs of dissolution.

224. How will our greatest success be achieved?

>   By a recognition of the fact that it is just as essential to give as to receive.

225. Why do financiers frequently meet with great success?
   Because they do their own thinking.

226. Why do the great majority in every country remain the docile and apparently willing tools of the few?
   Because they let the few do all their thinking for them.

227. What is the effect of concentrating upon sorrow and loss?
   More sorrow and more loss.

228. What is the effect of concentrating upon gain?
   More gain.

229. Is this principle used in the business world?
   It is the only principle which is ever used, or ever can be used; there is no other principle. The fact that it may be used unconsciously does not alter the situation.

230. What is the practical application of this principle?
   The fact that success is an effect, not a cause, and if we wish to secure the effect we must ascertain the cause, or idea or thought by which the effect is created.

231. Upon what principle does the theory and practice of every system of Metaphysics in existence depend?
> Upon a knowledge of the "Truth" concerning yourself and the world in which you life.

232. What is the "Truth" concerning yourself?
> The real "I" or ego is spiritual and can therefore never be less than perfect.

233. What is the method of destroying any form of error?
> To absolutely convince yourself of the "Truth" concerning the condition which you wish to see manifested.

234. Can we do this for others?
> The Universal Mind in which "we live and move and have our being" is one and indivisible, it is therefore just as possible to help others as to help ourselves.

235. What is the Universal Mind?
> The totality of all mind in existence.

236. Where is the Universal Mind?
> The Universal Mind is omnipresent, it exists everywhere. There is no place where it is not. It is therefore within us. It is "The World within." It is our spirit, our life.

237. What is the nature of the Universal Mind?

> It is spiritual and consequently creative. It seeks to express itself in form.

238. How may we act on the Universal Mind?

> Our ability to think is our ability to act on the Universal Mind and bring it into manifestation for the benefit of ourselves or others.

239. What is meant by thinking?

> Clear, decisive, calm, deliberate, sustained thought with a definite end in view.

240. What will be the result?

> You will also be able to say, "It is not I that doeth the works, but the 'Father' that dwelleth within me, He doeth the works." You will come to know that the "Father" is the Universal Mind and that He does really and truly dwell within you, in other words, you will come to know that the wonderful promises made in the Bible are fact, not fiction, and can be demonstrated by anyone having sufficient understanding.

Go Thunk Yourself!

Dr. Robert C. Worstell

Who is Dr. Robert C. Worstell?

Rev. Dr. Robert C. Worstell, M.Msc, PhD is an independent researcher and the author of several self-help and personal development books, Thinking at Internet Speed, How Self-Help Authors Write Bestsellers, Go Thunk Yourself™, Go Thunk Yourself, Again!, Go Thunk Yourself, S'more!, and Go Thunk Yourself, Compleat!,

He has also edited several publications: The Complete Thomas Troward Collection, Getting Rich, Being Healthy, Being Great, Think, Thank, Thunk!, and edited many self-help classics for republication. As well, he's edited and produced The Go Thunk Yourself Student Handbook and the Go Thunk Yourself Companion CD.

Worstell also maintains several blogs which support these books. He is perhaps the first to invite audience participation in writing several books, through posting the entire book to his blog and simultaneously publishing to the Print-on-Demand Publisher Lulu. This arrangement enables correction and updates to hardcopy versions within minutes.

He has certificates in Computer Networking and Wireless Broadband, as well as degrees in Marketing, Comparative Religions and Computer Science, with specialist studies in User Interfaces.

Worstell lives on a working farm in rural Missouri and is continually involved in research to improve the quality of life. He has spent over 35 years researching the human condition through personal studies of counseling, education, and self-improvement.

Other books in this series:

Go Thunk Yourself, Again!

There are reasons why you don't always think clearly or as fast as you'd like to. There are reasons why you haven't gotten the success, wealth, and happiness you've always dreamded of.

Following on the success of "Go Thunk Yourself!(TM)", this is a simple guide to thinking outside any box, learning how to swim through floods of data, and develop your own world view. In this book, learn the underlying laws that the universe runs on - and how to make these laws work for you! Here are the simple scientific and spiritual patterns which make or break success for any individual. By learning these patterns, **you can make your dreams become reality**.

Part of the Go Thunk Yourself Series.

Go Thunk Yourself, S'more!

Take your life in your own hands and create the world you've always dreamed of.

You learned techniques of improving your life in Go Thunk Yourself!. You studied how to use "Thunking" to free your mind and speed up your thought in Go Thunk Yourself, Again!.

Now, change your world view into one you've always dreamed of. You can re-program your mental computer to re-create yourself into a wealthier, healthier, and happier person - and **remain that way for the rest of your life!**

This book gives you the tools to **start your life anew**.

Dr. Robert C. Worstell

More Resources From this Author:

The Go Thunk Yourself Student Handbook

The student handbook which accompanies and completes the Go Thunk Yourself series.

This is used in conjunction with the earlier books in the Go Thunk Yourself series, or can be used alone. This handbook contains all the steps needed in the exact sequence which will place you firmly on the road to achieving your goals.

At full letter-size, with spiral binding and ample margins, this is a perfect study book – lots of room for highlighting and notes. Contains text by Wallace Wattles, Napoleon Hill, Charles F. Haanel, and Serge Kahili King.

Also now available in an inexpensive trade paperback size (perfect for studying over lunch).

Go Thunk Yourself Companion CD

Get the key referenced works from the Go Thunk Yourself books series, each compiled into PDF format for easy on-screen viewing. This CD contains all the beta versions of the three GTY books, as well as the masterworks of Haanel, Hill, Troward, Allen, Wattles, plus authors: Franklin, Ghazzali, Barnum, Clason, and many more.

Have all the references for your self-help studies in one place for ready reference.

Books in the Go Thunk Yourself Reference Library:

THINK, THANK, THUNK!

There are three authors who have completely changed your world -

Charles F. Haanel - "The Master Key System"
Wallace D. Wattles - "TheScience of Getting Rich"
Napoleon Hill - "Think and Grow Rich"

Every major self-help author and every true success on this planet all use the same underlying system. I cover this in "Go Thunk Yourself". This system as actual and underlying all that exists in our world - which is as we create it. From them, **you can work out the solution to any problem** - if you apply what they teach to yourself and your dreams.

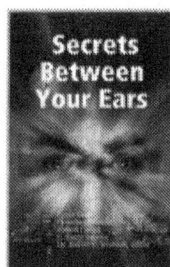

Secrets Between Your Ears

There is a way to re-program yourself to achieve the greatness you know is there.

Contained in this volume are three masterworks:
"Wake Up and Live!" by Dorothea Brande,
"The Secret of the Ages" by Robert Collier, and
"Self-Mastery and the Practice of Autosuggestion" by Emile Coue and C. Harry Brooks.

Within this text are the simple techniques (known and used by Napoleon Hill, author of "Think and Grow Rich") that will make it possible to acquire any amount of money, degree of happiness, and quality of health you desire.

Getting Rich, Being Well, Being Great

If you are familiar with the perennial bestselling classic, **The Science of Getting Rich**, you may or may not know that Wallace D. Wattles also wrote two other works which were meant to be following texts.

You can be rich, but you can also be healthy and you can also be great. **Read this book and you can be well on your way to getting everything you want in life**. By reading and comparing these three books in one volume, you will see how there are basic, underlying laws and principles at work in this universe - and you can put them to work for you.

The Complete Thomas Troward Collection

Thomas Troward is perhaps the single most influential writer in self-help. Napoleon Hill (Think and Grow Rich), Charles F. Haanel (The Master Key System) and many other authors either quote Troward directly or have been influenced by those who studied Troward's lectures and books.

This is a collection of his complete works, with a combined table of contents and easy-to-read format. A reference no professional or casual student of self-help should be without.

This is a key reference behind the successful Go Thunk Yourself! series.

View more resources at http://stores.lulu.com/robertworstell

Now what are you going to do?

I've given you all these tools to change your life. Now it's over to you.

In the bibliography is a list of books I've studied to achieve my conclusions. But this book is nothing unless you can use something from it. As in the first book: again, buy these other books and do your own research.

With the first book and now this one, you can change the way you think and handle life. I've distilled these data down to just a few. There are tons of examples laying around for you to find and prove them for yourself. But they won't (necessarily) rise up and bite you with understanding. The point is now that you should go and DO SOMETHING.

So get going and achieve your wealth, success and fame. There is no external force keeping you from achieving what you want in life. There are no victims in this universe. The only reasons you haven't already done so lie within yourself.

Good Hunting!

Dr. Robert C. Worstell

gothunkyourself.blogspot.com

http://gothunkyourself.com/

www.ingramcontent.com/pod-product-compliance
Lightning Source LLC
Chambersburg PA
CBHW032020230426
43671CB00005B/148